# THE ALCHEMIST

# THE ALCHEMIST

## Ben Jonson

a *Broadview Anthology of British Literature* edition

Contributing Editor, *The Alchemist*:
John Greenwood, St. Jerome's University

General Editors,
*Broadview Anthology of British Literature*:
Joseph Black, University of Massachusetts, Amherst
Leonard Conolly, Trent University
Kate Flint, University of Southern California
Isobel Grundy, University of Alberta
Don LePan, Broadview Press
Roy Liuzza, University of Tennessee
Jerome J. McGann, University of Virginia
Anne Lake Prescott, Barnard College
Barry V. Qualls, Rutgers University
Claire Waters, University of California, Davis

broadview press

Broadview Press – www.broadviewpress.com
Peterborough, Ontario, Canada

Founded in 1985, Broadview Press remains a wholly independent publishing house. Broadview's focus is on academic publishing: our titles are accessible to university and college students as well as scholars and general readers. With over 800 titles in print, Broadview has become a leading international publisher in the humanities, with world-wide distribution. Broadview is committed to environmentally responsible publishing and fair business practices.

Library and Archives Canada Cataloguing in Publication

Title: The alchemist / Ben Jonson ; contributing editor, The alchemist, John Greenwood, St.
   Jerome's University.
Names: Jonson, Ben, 1573?-1637, author. | Greenwood, John Philip Peter, 1951- editor.
Series: Broadview anthology of British literature edition.
Description: Series statement: Broadview anthology of British literature edition
Identifiers: Canadiana 20200160346 | ISBN 9781554813674 (softcover)
Subjects: LCGFT: Drama.
Classification: LCC PR2605.A2 G74 2020 | DDC 822/.3—dc23

*Broadview Press handles its own distribution in North America:*
PO Box 1243, Peterborough, Ontario, K9J 7H5, Canada
555 Riverwalk Parkway, Tonawanda, NY 14150, USA
Tel: (705) 743-8990; Fax: (705) 743-8353
email: customerservice@broadviewpress.com

For all territories outside of North America, distribution is handled by Eurospan Group.

Broadview Press acknowledges the financial
support of the Government of Canada
for our publishing activities.

Developmental Editor: Nora Ruddock
Cover Designer: Lisa Brawn
Typesetter: Alexandria Stuart

PRINTED IN CANADA

# Contents

# Contents

# Introduction

# Ben Jonson
## 1572–1637

B en Jonson was an innovator in poetry, drama, and criticism. In
1616 he became the first Englishman to edit and publish not just
his own poetry but his own drama. Like Shakespeare a pioneer in the
transition from verse to prose in comic dialogue, with a particular
talent for shaping social and moral satire into comedy, Jonson also
preferred to create his own plots rather than to borrow stories from
earlier sources. His reputation came to be partially eclipsed by that of
Shakespeare, for his humanist erudition and the frequent comic realism of his drama made him seem flat and pedantic beside what was
read as Shakespeare's genial inspiration (what Milton called his "native
woodnotes wild")—a writer for scholars, to be respected and admired
sooner than loved and enjoyed. The twentieth century, though, felt an
affinity for what appeared to be the anticipatory modern elements in
Jonson—his "plain style," his acute social observation, and his auda-
city in manipulating dramatic and classical conventions.

Jonson's grounding in the classics began in adolescence at Westminster School under the noted scholar and antiquarian William
Camden, a lifelong friend whom Jonson later praised as the teacher
"to whom I owe all that I am in arts." After brief stints as an appren-
tice bricklayer and a soldier, Jonson joined the developing theater
world as an actor. *Every Man in his Humour* (1598), in which Shakespeare acted, established Jonson as master of the new "comedy of
humors," which lampoons eccentricities of character. Jonson also
announced himself as an innovator with a mission. His prologue
to the play sets out what remained the core of his dramatic philosophy; in it he advocates direct and realistic language ("deeds and
language such as men do use") and a return to classical unities of
time and space, eschewing the elaborate fantasies and distortions
common in Elizabethan comedy and even more common in Jacobean romance and tragicomedy. A more satirical sequel, *Every Man*

*out of his Humour* (1599), proved so popular that Jonson took the unorthodox step of personally supervising its publication, thereby establishing a double precedent—the play as property of its author rather than of the acting company, and the popular stage play as literary document.

Jonson's high opinion of his art proved justified; his plays *Volpone* (1606) and *The Alchemist* (1610) remain two of the most esteemed comedies in British literature. *Volpone* chronicles a scheming miser's deception of a series of legacy hunters; in *The Alchemist*, various vain and gullible types are exploited by three servants posing as musicians in their master's absence. Both are comedies of intrigue, and in both Jonson set new standards in incisive, naturalistic dialogue and intricate plot construction. Jonson also scored hits with *Epicoene* (1612), a sportive exploration of sexual politics, and *Bartholomew Fair* (1614), a broad, slice-of-life portrait of London holiday street life. His attempts at tragedy, *Sejanus* (1603) and *Catiline* (1612), were judged too ponderous and pedantic, though Jonson was convinced his reading public would overleap what he saw as the deficiencies of his playgoing audiences. In the case of *Catiline*, he was right: though never a performance success, it was the most-quoted English play of the seventeenth century.

Posterity has since consigned Jonson's tragedies to relative obscurity but has shown increased regard for the limpid and clever verse he contributed to the Jacobean court masques. These were entertainments, commissioned to celebrate special events, that were danced and acted by members of the court. They featured increasingly elaborate costumes, scenery, and special effects, all designed by Jonson's collaborator, the court architect Inigo Jones. Such spectacles as the *Masque of Blackness* (1605) and the *Masque of Beauty* (1608) played off antique myths, providing a venue for Jonson to display his classical learning and sharpen his lyrical gifts. Jonson also introduced, in such flattering yet admonitory court masques as *Pleasure Reconciled to Virtue and Love Restored* (1612), the intriguing device of the "antimasque," a more rough-and-tumble moment with comic images of irrationality or grotesquerie that the surrounding masque both absorbs and exorcizes. Between them, Jonson and Jones took the masque from transitory amusement into a high art that in its multimedia form in some ways anticipates the opera and even film.

Jonson considered himself above all a poet. His poetry follows his dramas and masques in the 1616 folio of his collected works, which was the culmination of his career to that point, "the ripest of my studies." When, in his "Epistle to the Countess of Rutland" (1600), he introduced his "strange poems, which as yet / Had not their form touched by an English wit," Jonson was referring to such classical forms as the ode, epistle, epitaph, and epigram that he intended to revive or invigorate with a more crystalline yet colloquial style. His two best-loved lyrics, "To Celia" and "Drink to Me Only With Thine Eyes," written for *Volpone*, are not mere translations of Catullus and Philostrates; they are quintessentially Jonsonian, bringing to mind Oscar Wilde's assertion that Jonson "made the poets of Greece and Rome terribly modern."

These classical poetic genres were well suited to the intensely personal and yet social nature of Jonson's poetry, and it is here that his turbulent life and personality are reflected most vividly. We see in his many commissioned occasional pieces the cultivation of the aristocratic patronage on which he depended—as in "To Penshurst," his eloquent tribute to the estate of the Sidney family. We witness his capacity for generous friendship in his epigrams to John Donne and his preface to Shakespeare's First Folio, and his capacity for grief in the restrained eloquence of his epitaphs on his young son and infant daughter. We even glean hints of his legendary appetite for food and drink in "Inviting a Friend to Supper," which celebrates the sort of literary camaraderie Jonson found (and read about in his beloved Horace) in his early years, at the Mermaid Tavern, where he held court with a coterie of wits and fellow writers. Other early literary friends included Raleigh, Bacon, Chapman, Beaumont, and Fletcher, while later in his career, he mentored younger poets such as Herrick, Suckling, and Carew, presiding over a literary cult of sorts, the "sons [or sometimes 'tribe'] of Ben," at the Devil Tavern in the 1620s. Jonson had enemies, too; he could be vain, arrogant and quarrelsome, especially in defense of his literary principles and reputation. Indeed, in 1598 he got into a fight with an actor and killed him (a crime for which he was branded and sent for a while to prison, where he became a Catholic, though he reconverted to Protestantism some years later).

A royal pension bestowed on him in 1616 enabled Jonson to leave the stage and concentrate largely on his poetry. In 1618, he traveled to Scotland, where he visited the poet William Drummond, who left a record of their conversations and Jonson's often imperious opinions. The following year he was awarded an honorary M.A. from Oxford. Such triumphs and his "tribe" or "sons" notwithstanding, the 1620s brought a gradual decline in Jonson's health and fortunes. A fire destroyed his library, along with several manuscripts, in 1623. The death of King James in 1625 left him without a place at court, necessitating a return to the stage in 1626 with *The Staple of News*, a satire on the emerging newspaper business; it was not well-received. In fact, he was never again to attain success as a playwright; Dryden was later to refer to these late plays as "Jonson's dotages." His masque-writing career ended with the culmination in 1631 of a long-running feud with Inigo Jones. Even though disabled and confined to his house after a stroke in 1628, however, and though no longer the influential lion of his youth, Jonson did not lack for admirers or companionship. When he died in August 1637, most of London's literary and social elite attended his funeral.

Ben Jonson did not leave the world of letters as he found it. His assertion of ownership and careful editing of his own works affected the development of modern authorship and certainly influenced the publication of Shakespeare's First Folio. His satirical comedies provided a significant model for Restoration and eighteenth-century drama, and even for later comic writers in other genres such as Fielding and Dickens. In numerous justificatory prologues to his plays, and in his commonplace book, *Timber, or Discoveries*, he left behind a striking record of a writer's mind at work. And the muscular yet supple "plain style" of his poetry was pivotal in deflecting a late Elizabethan taste for the highly wrought and decorative towards a more direct and colloquial manner that became one major strand of late seventeenth-century (and modern) aesthetics.

## *The Alchemist*

In Ben Jonson's *The Alchemist*, we see the poet in his element as a comic satirist for the English stage. Known for his adherence to classical rhetorical principles, Jonson's plays are simultaneously revered yet often unread, as they are associated (somewhat unfairly) with erudite learning and pedantry. His great comedies, however, of which *The Alchemist* is one, sparkle with intelligence and wit, and have entertained audiences for centuries of successful stage performance. In the words of one of Jonson's contemporaries, Sidney Godolphin, Jonson was "the Muses' fairest light in no dark time ... the deepest, plainest, highest, clearest pen."

*The Alchemist* is typical of Jonson's plays in that it is realistic, satiric, local, and sharp, with "deeds and language such as men do use." This realism means that the characters speak in the conversational idioms of the day, which can be challenging for the modern reader, and which, in the case of *The Alchemist*, are complicated by the extensive use of alchemical jargon, not to mention the esoteric language of puritans and dueling manuals. The rewards of Jonson's plays, however, have long been appreciated and continue to compel admiration: Coleridge named *The Alchemist* one of the three "most perfect plots" in the history of literature, and Jonson has long been celebrated for his characterization, judgment, and wit. More recently, critic Rick Bowers has drawn attention to *The Alchemist*'s radical rejection of authority; he calls the play a "party that never ends" with a "wonky clockwork brilliance."[1]

*The Alchemist* is one of the most celebrated of early seventeenth century "city" or "citizen" comedies: dramas that offer a contemporary, urban, and usually satirical portrait of London life. With earthy language and a manic pace, much of the play's mirth is generated by the clash between high-minded values and the mercenary motives of the characters. Indeed, the name that Jonson gives to his main protagonist, Subtle, the alchemist and con man of the title, is itself suggestive of the author's sharp-eyed moral focus. The name, the very word used to describe the serpent who tempts Adam and Eve in Genesis, suggests the character's lineage as a literary descendent of the devil of the morality plays. Subtle's alchemical assistant, the disguised servant Face—a person whose face changes along with opportunity—also registers devilishly manipulative cunning. One of the pairs' victims, meanwhile, Sir Epicure Mammon, has a name

---

1   See Rick Bowers, *Radical Comedy in Early Modern England*, Ashgate, 2008, p. 97.

that alerts us to the moral implications of his orientation towards excessive worldly desires: An "Epicure" is a disciple of Epicurus, a Greek materialist philosopher that viewed pleasure as the highest good; "Mammon," often personified as a devil, is associated with greed, avarice, and desire for riches and wealth: "No one can serve two masters ... God and mammon," the Gospels of Matthew and Luke maintain. A character with such a name seems a ripe prize indeed for slick operators looking for a con.

All of the alchemist's victims seek self-aggrandizement. Sir Epicure Mammon, for instance, desires the so-called "philosopher's stone," a legendary substance thought to be able not only to convert base metals into gold but also to provide the elixir of life, the source of immortality. In alchemy, the Magnum Opus or "great work" was the effort of discovering this stone and harnessing its rumored magical properties. Although the search was once thought to have a legitimate theoretical basis, Jonson is more in league with Chaucer's earlier "Canon's Yeoman's Tale" in its suggestion that this pursuit is morally suspect. Indeed, it may even be dangerously deluded in its presumption to uncover the secrets of nature and attempt to evade and outdo them.

Somewhat unusually for English drama, the play adheres to the dictum of the "unities" derived from the work of Aristotle and embraced by many early modern playwrights on the European continent. *The Alchemist* displays the unity of time—the action takes place within a single day; the unity of place—the action takes place at one location; and the unity of action—all of the scenes contribute directly to the unfolding of the plot. Hemmed in by the smoky fumigated atmosphere of the plague-besieged city, the entire play takes place within, and just outside of, Lovewit's house, the owner of which has left town for the country to avoid disease. The house is in the London neighborhood of Blackfriars, where Jonson also lived—and where the play was written to be performed, at the Blackfriars Theatre, an indoor venue that had recently been acquired by the King's Men. An air of contemporary relevance also surrounds the incorporation of plague into the play's events: theaters would be closed later in the summer of 1610 due to a bout of plague that affected the city that year. With its specificity of time and place, Jonson's dramatic strategy in *The Alchemist* reflects the statement of his philosophy in the prologue to *Every Man in His Humor*, a play staged years earlier, which claims to present

> Deeds, and language, such as men do use,
> And persons, such as comedy would choose,
> When she would show an image of the times,
> And sport with human follies, not with crimes;
> Except we make 'em such, by loving still
> Our popular errors, when we know th' are ill.
> I mean such errors as you'll confess,
> By laughing at them, they deserve no less.

Though *The Alchemist* appears to have been performed at Blackfriars sometime in or around 1610—either in July, just before the closure of the London theaters, or in late 1610 or early 1611 after their reopening—its first recorded performance was in September 1610, at Oxford, while the King's Men were touring during the closure. While the play was immediately successful, it also drew criticism from some of the scholars at Oxford, who objected to Jonson's use of scripture for satirical purposes in his ridicule of the Puritans. But even one such scholar, Henry Jackson, notes in his condemnation of the biblical satire that the company "performed to great applause," and *The Alchemist* was quickly recognized as one of Jonson's best plays. It was soon performed at court, and it remained in the repertory of the King's Men until the theaters were closed in 1649.

Throughout the seventeenth century, when Jonson's reputation as a playwright stood beyond even Shakespeare's, *The Alchemist* was frequently seen as his crowning achievement. This reputation continued into the eighteenth century; Richard Steele commented, after attending a performance of *The Alchemist* in 1709, that it "is an example of Ben's extensive genius and penetration into the passions and follies of mankind." As the play's contemporary idioms and alchemical jargon became more challenging for eighteenth-century audiences, however, the play began to be adapted for performance. The famed actor David Garrick (1717–79) took the role of Abel Drugger in 1743, performing it until 1776, and he adapted the play to make this role central, minimizing the roles of Face and Subtle. This version of the play was very popular, and Garrick's adaptation was eventually turned into a version by Francis Gentleman entitled *The Tobacconist*; these adaptations produced an *Alchemist* that was more conventional and morally palatable to the audiences of the day.

Discomfort with the bawdiness and biting satire of *The Alchemist* kept it from being frequently staged in the nineteenth century. The twentieth century, however, saw renewed scholarly interest in *The Alchemist*, with several important editions of the text being produced, as well as increased numbers of performances on the stage. The twenty-first century continues to bring diverse critical attention to the play, with an emphasis on historicist readings, and with particular attention to subjects such as Jonson's depiction of gender roles, his use of metatheatricality, and the complex array of moral positions audiences may find in the play. *The Alchemist*'s ruthless uncovering of greed as a dominant and perennial motivation for human action continues to find wide traction, both for readers and stage audiences alike.

## Alchemy

Martin Luther, in his *Table Talk*, said of alchemy that he "likes [it] very well ... not only for the profits it brings in melting metals, in decocting, preparing, extracting and distilling herbs, roots; ... [but] also for the sake of the allegory and secret signification, which is exceedingly fine, touching the resurrection of the dead at the last day." Alchemy in early modern Europe (and England) included both the practical arts of metallurgy and natural medicine, as well as an allegorical language that spoke of spiritual mysteries to the initiated. While Jonson satirizes its jargon and the motives of some of its practitioners, alchemy itself was part of a way of interpreting the world that was very much accepted by most medieval and early modern scholars, including Thomas Aquinas and John Newton. Elizabeth I had a Court Magus, John Dee, who, in addition to being a respected mathematician, was also an astrologer and alchemist seeking the philosopher's stone. Jonson himself could cast astrological charts (though apparently he did not put much stock in them).

The alchemical tradition seems to have originated separately in the Middle East and China, with the two traditions beginning to influence each other somewhere around the tenth century. The Chinese tradition placed emphasis on the search for the philosopher's stone, an emphasis that was brought into the Arabic tradition once the two had contact. Alchemy surfaced in Western Europe in the twelfth century, when Robert of Chester translated the *Book of the Composition of Alchemy* from Arabic into Latin; soon, more translations were undertaken, and the study of alchemy spread throughout the Middle Ages. In Europe, the practice combined practical metallurgy with occult interests in the nature of matter, God, and the universe; the latter interests were expressed in allegorical language derived from Greek philosophy, Muslim and Chinese lore, Christianity, and mystery religions. This obscure language also served to keep valuable metallurgical recipes secret from the uninitiated.

The central principle in alchemy is a physical and spiritual process by which base materials are purified, or "perfected." Matter itself is seen as an undifferentiated mass, distinguished into "bodies" by consisting of varying degrees of the four elements (fire, water, air, earth), which appear in the form of the "tria prima" or "three principles" of sulfur, mercury, and salt. Fire is considered dry and hot; Air is hot and moist; Water is moist and cold; and Earth is cold and dry. The elements are also hierarchical, with Fire being highest and Earth lowest. Alchemy sees the world through hierarchical "correspondences" between the cosmic bodies, the natural world, the state, and human life (known as "the great chain of being," which links everything from God to the smallest inanimate particle). Anything within the chain can be understood as a metaphor or metonymy for other things, and the macrocosm has sympathetic connections to the microcosm: so, for example, a hair from a person in the hands of a witch could be used to affect the body from which it came. Humankind, in the great chain, makes the crucial link from animal life to the angelic, from the natural world to the spiritual.

Alchemical experiments had the aim of achieving pure metals (and, ultimately, of achieving the philosopher's stone, which would not only turn baser metals to gold but bring enlightenment and immortality). Using many vessels of different shapes, and using a variety of heats and ovens, the alchemist sought to perfect what was imperfect, and to reverse the decay to which all matter in a fallen world is subject. These practical experiments of metallurgy and chemistry also had spiritual significance for the practitioner, purifying the soul for eventual immortality. The processes for perfecting metals were extremely varied, and the language opaque, with each component being described in many different ways and interpreted on different allegorical levels. Mercury, for example, is variously described as a running deer, a white woman, quicksilver, rain, a dragon, a hermaphrodite, and a mermaid, among other things. According to Paracelsus (1493–1541), an influential Swiss alchemist, "quicksilver" was one of seven metals, each of which corresponded to one of seven "wandering planets": quicksilver corresponded to Mercury, gold to the Sun, silver to the Moon, copper to Venus, tin to Jupiter, iron to Mars, and lead to Saturn. These correspondences linked alchemy with astrology, which brought elements of prognostication to the experiments and processes.

While the theory behind alchemy was accepted by most, the obscurity and secrecy surrounding its processes, as well as its promises of immortality and wealth, made it a tempting means to cheat others, and such gulling became so common that "to use the craft of multiplication of gold and silver" became a felony in 1403. Nonetheless, alchemy remained a "science" with many adherents, even royal ones, as they sought to renew the country's coffers with gold: Henry VI ordered three different reports on whether alchemy could produce gold, and Elizabeth I believed in the possibility, hiring alchemists to attempt transmutation. Belief in alchemy continued through the seventeenth century, dwindling only in the eighteenth, as the scientific revolution revealed much of it to be without scientific basis. In some circles, however, occult interest in alchemy has continued to flourish; W.B. Yeats and Carl Jung, for example, were both interested in alchemical texts and what they could reveal about human consciousness.

**Note on the Text**

This text of *The Alchemist* is based on the 1616 Folio version, which was overseen by Jonson and included changes to punctuation and added stage directions. We are indebted to both the Revels edition of 1967, edited by F.H. Mares, and the modern spelling version of the Cambridge edition of 2012, edited by Peter Holland and William Sherman.

# *The Alchemist*

## To the Lady, Most Deserving Her Name and Blood: Mary, Lady Wroth[1]

Madam,

In the age of sacrifices, the truth of religion was not in the greatness and fat of the offerings, but in the devotion and zeal of the sacrificers: else, what could a handful of gums have done in the sight of a *hecatomb*?[2] Or, how might I appear at this altar, except with those affections, that no less love the light and witness, than they have the conscience of your virtue? If what I offer bear an acceptable odour, and hold the first strength, it is your value of it, which remembers where, when, and to whom it was kindled. Otherwise, as the times are, there comes rarely forth that thing, so full of authority or example, but by assiduity and custom, grows less and loses. This, yet, safe in your judgment (which is a Sidney's) is forbidden to speak more; lest it talk or look like one of the ambitious faces of the time, who, the more they paint,[3] are the less themselves.

Your Ladyship's true honourer,

Ben. Jonson.

## To the Reader[4]

If thou beest more, thou art an understander,[5] and then I trust thee. If thou art one that takest up, and but a pretender, beware at what hands thou receivest thy commodity;[6] for thou wert never more fair in the

---

1  *Mary, Lady Wroth*  Well-known poet (1587–1651/3) from an aristocratic literary family; she was the daughter of Robert Sidney and the niece of Sir Philip Sidney. She and Jonson were friends. The title of the dedication puns on her name, pronounced "Worth."

2  *gums*  I.e., incense;  *hecatomb*  In Ancient Greece and Rome, a large public sacrifice of many animals.

3  *paint*  Put on makeup.

4  *To the Reader*  Included in the 1612 Quarto but not in the 1616 Folio edition of the *Works*.

5  *understander*  One who understands; can also refer to theatergoers standing on the ground, lower than the stage.

6  *takest up*  Buys;  *pretender*  One who pretends to know, but also one who accepts the terms of a swindle;  *commodity*  Merchandise.

way to be cozened[1] (than in this age) in *poetry*, especially in plays: wherein, now, the concupiscence of dances and antics[2] so reigneth, as to run away from Nature, and be afraid of her, is the only point of art that tickles the *spectators*. But how out of purpose and place, do I name Art? When the professors are grown so obstinate contemners of it, and presumers on their own naturals,[3] as they are deriders of all diligence that way, and, by simple mocking at the terms, when they understand not the things, think to get off wittily with their ignorance. Nay, they are esteemed the more learned and sufficient for this, by the many, through their excellent vice[4] of judgment. For they commend writers as they do fencers or wrestlers, who if they come in robustiously, and put for it with a great deal of violence, are received for the braver fellows, when many times their own rudeness is the cause of their disgrace, and a little touch of their adversary gives all that boisterous force the foil.[5] I deny not, but that these men, who always seek to do more than enough, may some time happen on some thing that is good and great; but very seldom: and when it comes it doth not recompense the rest of their ill.[6] It sticks out, perhaps, and is more eminent, because all is sordid and vile about it: as lights are more discerned in a thick darkness than a faint shadow. I speak not this out of a hope to do good to any man against his will; for I know, if it were put to the question[7] of theirs and mine, the worse would find more suffrages, because the most favour common errors. But I give thee this warning, that there is a great difference between those that (to gain the opinion of copy) utter all they can, however unfitly, and those that use election and a mean.[8] For it is only the disease of the unskilful, to think rude things greater than polished, or scattered more numerous[9] than composed.

---

1   *cozened*   Duped, cheated.

2   *concupiscence*   Sensual desire;   *antics*   Pageants, or grotesque gestures.

3   *professors*   Critics and writers who make literature their profession, or those who "profess" to be writers;   *contemners*   Despisers;   *naturals*   Natural talents.

4   *vice*   Fault or viciousness.

5   *robustiously*   Boisterously, noisily;   *for the braver*   As the more daring;   *rudeness*   Forcefulness; also lack of wit or ability;   *foil*   Defeat.

6   *their ill*   I.e., what they have done badly.

7   *question*   Vote.

8   *opinion of copy*   Reputation for abundance of language;   *election and a mean*   Judgment and restraint.

9   *numerous*   Many, but also referring to the "numbers" of measured verse, hence "harmonious."

## The Persons of the Play

Subtle, *the alchemist*
Face, *the housekeeper*
Doll[1] Common, *their colleague*
Dapper, *a clerk*
Drugger, *a tobacco-man*
Lovewit, *master of the house*
Sir Epicure Mammon, *a knight*
Pertinax[2] Surly, *a gamester*
Tribulation Wholesome, *a pastor of Amsterdam*
Ananias, *a deacon there*
Kastril, *the angry boy*[3]
Dame Pliant, *his sister, a widow*
Neighbours, Officers, Mutes

(*The Scene: London*)

## The Argument

T he sickness hot,[4] a master quit, for fear,
H is house in town, and left one servant there.
E ase him corrupted, and gave means to know
A cheater and his punk,° who, now brought low,        *harlot*
L eaving their narrow practice, were become        5
C oz'ners° at large: and only wanting some        *cheats*
H ouse to set up, with him they here contract,[5]
E ach for a share, and all begin to act.
M uch company they draw, and much abuse,
I n casting figures,° telling fortunes, news,        *horoscopes*  10
S elling of flies, flat bawdry, with the stone:[6]
T ill it, and they, and all in *fume*° are gone.        *smoke*

---

1  *Doll*  Slang term for a prostitute.
2  *Pertinax*  Latin: stubborn.
3  *Kastril*  Alternate spelling of "kestrel," a small hawk, used figuratively in Jonson's day to express contempt; *angry boy*  Young man given to drunken, boisterous behavior.
4  *sickness hot*  Raging plague. The plague epidemic was particularly severe in 1610, the year *The Alchemist* was first performed.
5  *contract*  Strike a bargain.
6  *flies*  Familiar spirits; *flat bawdry*  Unmitigated prostitution; *stone*  Philosopher's stone, a mythical substance granting wealth and eternal life.

Fortune, that favours fools, these two short hours
We wish away; both for your sakes, and ours,
Judging Spectators: and desire in place,[1]
To th' Author justice, to ourselves but grace.
Our Scene is London, 'cause we would make known,       5
No country's mirth is better than our own.
No clime breeds better matter, for your whore,
Bawd, squire,° impostor, many persons more,                      *pimp*
Whose manners, now called humours,[2] feed the stage:
And which have still° been subject for the rage               *always*          10
Or spleen of comic writers. Though this pen
Did never aim to grieve, but better° men,                         *improve*
Howe'er the age he lives in doth endure
The vices that she breeds, above their cure.
But, when the wholesome remedies are sweet,                    15
And, in their working, gain and profit meet,
He hopes to find no spirit so much diseased,
But will, with such fair correctives, be pleased:
For here, he doth not fear who can apply.[3]
If there be any, that will sit so nigh                               20
Unto the stream, to look what it doth run,
They shall find things they'd think, or wish, were done;
They are so natural follies, but so shown,
As even the doers may see, and yet not own.

---

1  *in place*  Instead.
2  *humours*  The four basic human temperaments, based on classical theory concerning the
   relative balance of four bodily fluids: blood, phlegm, yellow bile, and black bile.
3  *apply*  Attribute these vices (to individual audience members).

## ACT I, SCENE I

([*Enter*] *Face,* [*his sword drawn,*] *Subtle* [*holding a vial, and*] *Doll Common.*)

FACE. Believe 't, I will.

SUBTLE.                    Thy worst. I fart at thee.

DOLL. Ha' you your wits? Why, gentlemen! For love—

FACE. Sirrah,[1] I'll strip you—

SUBTLE.                    What to do? Lick figs°      *hemorrhoids*

Out at my—

FACE.            Rogue, rogue, out of all your sleights.[2]

DOLL. Nay, look ye! Sovereign, General, are you madmen?      5

SUBTLE. O, let the wild sheep loose. I'll gum your silks[3]

With good strong water,° and° you come.      *acid / if*

DOLL.                              Will you have

The neighbours hear you? Will you betray all?

Hark, I hear somebody.

FACE.                    Sirrah–

SUBTLE.                    I shall mar

All that the tailor has made, if you approach.      10

FACE. You most notorious whelp, you insolent slave.

Dare you do this?

SUBTLE.            Yes, faith, yes faith.

FACE.                              Why! Who

Am I, my mongrel? Who am I?

SUBTLE.                    I'll tell you,

Since you know not yourself—

FACE.                    Speak lower, rogue.

SUBTLE. Yes. You were once (time's not long past) the good,      15

Honest, plain, livery-three-pound-thrum;[4] that kept

Your master's worship's house, here, in the Friars,[5]

---

1  *Sirrah*  Term of address that expresses the speaker's contempt, the addressee's social inferiority, or both.
2  *out of all your sleights*  Stop all your deceitful tricks.
3  *gum your silks*  Ruin your clothes.
4  *livery-three-pound-thrum*  Poorly paid and poorly dressed servant.
5  *Friars*  Blackfriars district in London.

For the vacations[1]—

FACE.                    Will you be so loud?

SUBTLE.  Since, by my means, translated suburb-captain.[2]

20 FACE.  By your means, Doctor dog!

SUBTLE.                    Within man's memory,
    All this, I speak of.

FACE.                    Why, I pray you, have I
    Been countenanced° by you? Or you, by me?          *supported*
    Do but collect,° sir, where I met you first.          *recollect*

SUBTLE.  I do not hear well.

FACE.                    Not of this, I think it.

25 But I shall put you in mind, sir; at Pie-corner,[3]
    Taking your meal of steam in, from cooks' stalls,
    Where, like the father of hunger, you did walk
    Piteously costive,° with your pinched-horn nose,[4]          *constipated*
    And your complexion, of the Roman wash,[5]

30 Stuck full of black and melancholic worms,
    Like powder corns[6] shot at th' artillery yard.

SUBTLE.  I wish you could advance your voice[7] a little.

FACE.  When you went pinned up, in the several rags
    Y' had raked and picked from dunghills, before day,

35 Your feet in mouldy slippers, for your kibes,[8]
    A felt of rug,[9] and a thin threaden° cloak,          *threadbare*
    That scarce would cover your no-buttocks–

SUBTLE.                    So, sir!

FACE.  When all your alchemy, and your algebra,
    Your minerals, vegetals, and animals,

40 Your conjuring, coz'ning, and your dozen of trades,

---

1  *vacations*  Times when the courts were not in session.
2  *translated*  Promoted, or moved to a new career;  *suburb-captain*  Head of a disreputable
    district, perhaps a pimp or brothel head.
3  *Pie-Corner*  Area of Smithfield known for its shops selling prepared food.
4  *pinched-horn nose*  Nose in the shape of a shoe-horn, narrow and "pinched" from hunger.
5  *of the Roman wash*  Probably dark-colored (like an Italian) or red (in reference to the
    Catholic Church).
6  *worms ... powder corns*  Blackheads, like grains of gunpowder.
7  *advance your voice*  Raise your voice.
8  *kibes*  Chilblains, inflammation of the hands and feet from exposure to cold.
9  *felt of rug*  Coarse woolen hat.

Could not relieve your corps° with so much linen      *body*
Would make you tinder, but to see a fire;
I ga' you countenance, credit for your coals,
Your stills,[1] your glasses, your materials,
Built you a furnace, drew you customers,      45
Advanced all your black arts; lent you, beside,
A house to practise in—
SUBTLE.                              Your master's house?
FACE. Where you have studied the more thriving skill
  Of bawdry since.
SUBTLE.                    Yes, in your master's house.
  You, and the rats, here kept possession.      50
  Make it not strange.[2] I know y' were one could keep
  The butt'ry-hatch° still locked, and save the chippings,[3]      *pantry*
  Sell the dole beer to aqua-vitae men,[4]
  The which, together with your Christmas vails°      *tips*
  At post-and-pair,° your letting out of counters,[5]      *card game* 55
  Made you a pretty stock, some twenty marks,[6]
  And gave you credit, to converse with cobwebs,
  Here, since your mistress's death hath broke up house.
FACE. You might talk softlier, rascal.
SUBTLE.                              No, you scarab,°      *dung-beetle*
  I'll thunder you in pieces. I will teach you      60
  How to beware to tempt a Fury[7] again,
  That carries tempest in his hand and voice.
FACE. The place has made you valiant.
SUBTLE.                              No, your clothes.
  Thou vermin, have I ta'en thee out of dung,
  So poor, so wretched, when no living thing      65
  Would keep thee company, but a spider, or worse?

---

1  *stills*  Equipment for distillation.
2  *Make it ... strange*  Don't pretend you don't know what I'm talking about.
3  *chippings*  Stale bread that would usually be given away as charity.
4  *dole beer*  Leftover beer usually given out to the poor;  *aqua-vitae men*  Sellers of strong
   liquor (aqua-vitae), who could redistill the beer into a stronger beverage for resale.
5  *letting out of counters*  Supplying counting chips (for the card game). Whoever supplied the
   chips took a cut from the pot.
6  *marks*  A mark is a measure of gold weight (about 8 ounces of gold).
7  *Fury*  Classical goddess of vengeance.

Raised thee from brooms, and dust, and wat'ring-pots?
Sublimed thee, and exalted thee, and fixed thee
In the third region, called our state of grace?[1]
70   Wrought thee to spirit, to quintessence,[2] with pains
Would twice have won me the philosopher's work?[3]
Put thee in words and fashion? Made thee fit
For more than ordinary fellowships?
Giv'n thee thy oaths, thy quarrelling dimensions,[4]
75   Thy rules to cheat at horse-race, cock-pit, cards,
Dice, or whatever gallant tincture[5] else?
Made thee a second in mine own great art?
And have I this for thank? Do you rebel?
Do you fly out i' the projection?[6]
80   Would you be gone now?
DOLL.                   Gentlemen, what mean you?
Will you mar all?
SUBTLE.            Slave, thou hadst had no name—
DOLL.  Will you undo yourselves, with civil war?
SUBTLE.  Never been known, past *equi clibanum*,[7]
The heat of horse-dung, under ground, in cellars,
85   Or an ale-house, darker than Deaf John's:[8] been lost
To all mankind, but laundresses and tapsters,°           *barkeeps*
Had not I been.
DOLL.            Do you know who hears you, Sovereign?
FACE.  Sirrah—
DOLL.           Nay, General, I thought you were civil—

---

1  *Sublimed thee ... state of grace*  Subtle describes his transformation of Face in alchemical terms: Sublimation converts solids to vapor by heat; exaltation raises substances to a higher degree of purity or concentration; fixation deprives substances of their fluidity; and the "third region" is the highest and purest region of air.

2  *quintessence*  In alchemical terms, the fifth "essence," which can be extracted through distillation, and which can transform the other four elements.

3  *philosopher's work*  Philosopher's stone.

4  *quarrelling dimensions*  Rules for quarreling.

5  *tincture*  In alchemy, a transformative substance.

6  *fly out*  Explode; *projection*  Final stage of the alchemical process, when success is imminent.

7  *equi clibanum*  Latin: horse dung, which is burned as a heat source for some alchemical procedures.

8  *Deaf John's*  An unknown (and likely quite seedy) tavern.

FACE.  I shall turn desperate, if you grow thus loud.
SUBTLE.  And hang thyself, I care not.                                          90
FACE.                                                    Hang thee, collier,[1]
  And all thy pots, and pans, in picture,[2] I will,
  Since thou hast moved me—
DOLL.                                    O, this'll o'erthrow all.
FACE.  Write thee up bawd, in Paul's;[3] have all thy tricks
  Of coz'ning with a hollow coal,[4] dust, scrapings,
  Searching for things lost, with a sieve and shears,[5]                        95
  Erecting figures in your rows of houses,°                        *zodiac signs*
  And taking in of shadows with a glass,°                          *crystal ball*
  Told in red letters; and a face cut° for thee,                   *woodcut*
  Worse than Gamaliel Ratsey's.[6]
DOLL.                                    Are you sound?°           *sane, healthy*
  Ha' you your senses, masters?                                                 100
FACE.                                    I will have
  A book, but barely reckoning thy impostures,
  Shall prove a true philosopher's stone,[7] to printers.
SUBTLE.  Away, you trencher-rascal!°                               *glutton*
FACE.                                    Out, you dog-leech![8]
  The vomit of all prisons—
DOLL.                                    Will you be
  Your own destructions, gentlemen?                                            105
FACE.                                    Still spewed out
  For lying too heavy o' the basket.[9]
SUBTLE.                                    Cheater.
FACE.                                    Bawd.

---

1  *collier*  One who carries coals; there is also a pun on "collar," which can refer to the hangman's noose. Subtle's alchemical work also requires a great deal of coal.
2  *in picture*  In a publicly posted image (i.e., one that would expose Subtle as a magician).
3  *in Paul's*  In St. Paul's Cathedral, the aisles of which were favorite places to post notices.
4  *coz'ning with a hollow coal*  An alchemist's trick, which involves hiding molten precious
   metal in the middle of a piece of charcoal so that, when burned, it appears to be transformed.
5  *sieve and shears*  Proverbial tools of divination to point to lost objects.
6  *Gamaliel Ratsey*  Infamous highwayman who robbed while wearing a hideous mask.
7  *Shall prove ... stone*  Shall be such a successful book that it will match the fortunes to be
   gained from the philosopher's stone.
8  *dog-leech*  Ignorant quack doctor; can also refer to veterinarians.
9  *lying too heavy o' the basket*  Eating more than one's share of the prison food.

SUBTLE. Cow-herd.

FACE.             Conjurer.

SUBTLE.                   Cut-purse.

FACE.                                 Witch.

DOLL.                                   O me!

    We are ruined! Lost! Ha' you no more regard

    To your reputations? Where's your judgment? 'Slight,°   *by God's light*

110  Have yet some care of me, o' your republic¹—

FACE.  Away this brach!° I'll bring thee, rogue, within         *bitch*

    The statute of sorcery, *tricesimo tertio*

    Of Harry the eight:² ay, and perhaps thy neck

    Within a noose, for laund'ring gold, and barbing it.³

115 DOLL. You'll bring your head within a cockscomb,° will you?  *fool's hat*

*She catcheth out Face his sword, and breaks Subtle's glass.*

    And you, sir, with your menstrue,° gather it up.         *solvent*

    'Sdeath,⁴ you abominable pair of stinkards,

    Leave off your barking, and grow one again,

    Or, by the light that shines, I'll cut your throats.

120  I'll not be made a prey unto the marshal,°           *prison officer*

    For ne'er a snarling dog-bolt° o' you both.            *scoundrel*

    Have you together cozen'd all this while,

    And all the world, and shall it now be said,

    You've made most courteous shift to cozen yourselves?

125  [*To Face.*] You will accuse him? You will bring him in

    Within the statute? Who shall take your word?

    A whoreson, upstart, apocryphal° captain,           *phony*

    Whom not a puritan in Blackfriars will trust

    So much as for a feather!⁵ [*To Subtle.*] And you, too,

130  Will give the cause, forsooth? You will insult,

---

1  *republic*  Common interest, with a pun implying that Doll is a "*res publica*" (Latin: common thing).

2  *statute of sorcery … Harry the eight*  Statute forbidding sorcery, passed in the thirty-third year (*tricesimo tertio*) of Henry VIII's reign; it was renewed under James I.

3  *laund'ring … barbing it*  Washing coins in acid and clipping their edges, both means of obtaining gold. Defacing currency was a capital offence.

4  *'Sdeath*  An oath, "God's death."

5  *feather*  Puritans in Blackfriars sold feathers as clothing ornaments.

And claim a primacy in the divisions?
You must be chief? As if you only had
The powder to project with,[1] and the work
Were not begun out of equality?
The venture tripartite? All things in common?                    135
Without priority? 'Sdeath! you perpetual curs,
Fall to your couples again, and cozen kindly,[2]
And heartily, and lovingly, as you should,
And lose not the beginning of a term,[3]
Or, by this hand, I shall grow factious too,                     140
And take my part,° and quit you.                    *share*

FACE.                                    'Tis his fault;
He ever murmurs, and objects his pains,
And says, the weight of all lies upon him.

SUBTLE.    Why, so it does.

DOLL.                    How does it? Do not we
Sustain our parts?                                                145

SUBTLE.            Yes, but they are not equal.

DOLL.  Why, if your part exceed today, I hope
Ours may, tomorrow, match it.

SUBTLE.                    Ay, they may.

DOLL.  May, murmuring mastiff? Ay, and do. Death on me!
[*To Face.*]  Help me to throttle him.

SUBTLE.                    Dorothy! mistress Dorothy,
'Ods precious,[4] I'll do anything. What do you mean?            150

DOLL.  Because o' your fermentation and cibation?[5]

SUBTLE.  Not I, by heaven—

DOLL.                    Your *Sol* and *Luna*[6]— [*To Face.*] Help me.

SUBTLE.  Would I were hanged then? I'll conform myself.

DOLL.  Will you, sir? Do so then, and quickly: swear.

---

1   *powder to project with*   Ground philosopher's stone, with a pun on "project," meaning both to
    scheme and to throw powdered philosopher's stone into a crucible (as a means of making gold).
2   *Fall to your couples*   Join together;   *kindly*   A pun: "kindly" means not only "affection-
    ately," but also "naturally" and "like kin."
3   *term*   Period during which law courts were in session; a busy social season.
4   *'Ods precious*   An oath, "God's precious blood."
5   *fermentation and cibation*   Late stages of alchemy.
6   *Sol and Luna*   Gold (sun) and silver (moon). In alchemy, each planet is associated with a
    metal.

155 SUBTLE. What should I swear?
DOLL.                    To leave your faction,° sir,        *quarrel*
   And labour, kindly, in the common work.
SUBTLE. Let me not breathe if I meant aught beside.
   I only used those speeches, as a spur
   To him.
DOLL.      I hope we need no spurs, sir. Do we?
160 FACE. 'Slid,[1] prove to-day, who shall shark° best.        *cheat*
SUBTLE.                              Agreed.
DOLL. Yes, and work close, and friendly.
SUBTLE.                      'Slight, the knot
   Shall grow the stronger, for this breach, with me.
DOLL. Why so, my good baboons! Shall we go make
   A sort° of sober, scurvy, precise° neighbours,    *group / puritanical*
165 (That scarce have smiled twice, sin' the king came in,[2])
   A feast of laughter at our follies? Rascals,
   Would run themselves from breath, to see me ride,[3]
   Or you t' have but a hole, to thrust your heads in,[4]
   For which you should pay ear-rent?[5] No, agree.
170 And may Don Provost[6] ride a feasting, long,
   In his old velvet jerkin and stained scarfs,
   (My noble Sovereign, and worthy General,)
   Ere we contribute a new crewel garter[7]
   To his most worsted worship.[8]
SUBTLE.                   Royal Doll!
175 Spoken like Claridiana,[9] and thyself!
FACE. For which at supper, thou shalt sit in triumph,
   And not be styled Doll Common, but Doll Proper,

---

1  *'Slid*  An oath, "By God's eyelid."
2  *came in*  I.e., was crowned; King James I was crowned in 1603.
3  *ride*  Carted through the streets in punishment as a prostitute.
4  *have but ... heads in*  Be put in the stocks.
5  *pay ear-rent*  Have your ears clipped.
6  *Don Provost*  Public executioner, who took clothes from those he executed.
7  *crewel garter*  Garter made of worsted (a fine woolen fabric), with a pun on "cruel" suggestive of a hangman's noose.
8  *his most worsted worship*  The executioner, with a pun on "worsted," meaning both "woolen fabric" and "defeated."
9  *Claridiana*  Heroine of *The Mirror of Knighthood*, a romance (first English edition 1578).

Doll Singular: the longest cut° at night,        *winning draw*
Shall draw thee for his Doll Particular.[1]

*[A bell rings.]*

SUBTLE. Who's that? One rings. To the window, Doll. Pray heav'n,   180
  The master do not trouble us, this quarter.°        *season*
FACE. O, fear not him. While there dies one a week
  O' the plague, he's safe, from thinking toward London.
  Beside, he's busy at his hop-yards,[2] now;
  I had a letter from him. If he do,        185
  He'll send such word, for airing of the house,
  As you shall have sufficient time, to quit it:
  Though we break up a fortnight, 'tis no matter.
SUBTLE. Who is it, Doll?
DOLL.          A fine young quodling.°        *green youth*
FACE.                           O,
  My lawyer's clerk, I lighted on last night,        190
  In Holborn, at the Dagger.[3] He would have
  (I told you of him) a familiar,[4]
  To rifle° with at horses, and win cups.        *gamble*
DOLL. O, let him in.
SUBTLE.        Stay. Who shall do't?
FACE.                    Get you
  Your robes on. I will meet him, as going out.        195
DOLL. And what shall I do?
FACE.          Not be seen, away.

*[Exit Doll.]*

---

1  *Common ... Particular*  This passage puns on grammatical terms (common, proper, singular, and particular) with implied sexual innuendo.
2  *hop-yards*  Lands given to the cultivation of hops.
3  *Holborn*  District of London; *Dagger*  Famous tavern.
4  *familiar*  Assisting spirit (here, one that assists with success in gambling).

Seem you very reserved.
SUBTLE.                          Enough.
FACE.                                    God be wi' you, sir,
  I pray you, let him know that I was here.
  His name is Dapper. I would gladly have stayed, but—


## ACT 1, SCENE 2


DAPPER. [*Within.*]  Captain, I am here.
FACE.                          Who's that? He's come, I think, Doctor.


[*Enter Dapper.*]

  Good faith, sir, I was going away.
DAPPER.                                In truth,
  I am very sorry, Captain.
FACE.                          But I thought
  Sure, I should meet you.
DAPPER.                          Ay, I'm very glad.
5  I had a scurvy writ, or two, to make,
  And I had lent my watch last night, to one
  That dines, today, at the sheriff's: and so was robbed
  Of my pastime.° Is this the cunning-man?°       *watch / conjurer*
FACE.  This is his worship.
DAPPER.                          Is he a doctor?
FACE.                                    Yes.
10 DAPPER.  And ha' you broke with[1] him, Captain?
FACE.                                                Ay.
DAPPER.                                        And how?
FACE.  Faith, he does make the matter, sir, so dainty°      *finicky*
  I know not what to say—
DAPPER.                          Not so, good Captain.
FACE.  Would I were fairly rid on't, believe me.
DAPPER.  Nay, now you grieve me, sir. Why should you wish so?
15  I dare assure you, I'll not be ungrateful.

---

1  *broke with*  Asked.

FACE. I cannot think you will, sir. But the law
 Is such a thing—and then he says, Read's matter[1]
 Falling so lately—
DAPPER.                    Read? He was an ass,
 And dealt, sir, with a fool.
FACE.                              It was a clerk, sir.
DAPPER. A clerk?                                                    20
FACE.                Nay, hear me, sir, you know the law
 Better, I think—
DAPPER. ·                I should, sir, and the danger.
 You know I showed the statute to you.
FACE.                                          You did so.
DAPPER. And will I tell, then? By this hand, of flesh,
 Would it might never write good court-hand[2] more,
 If I discover.[3] What do you think of me,                        25
 That I am a *Chiaus*?[4]
FACE.                  What's that?
DAPPER.                        The Turk was, here—
 As one would say, do you think I am a Turk?
FACE. I'll tell the Doctor so.
DAPPER.                    Do, good sweet Captain.
FACE. Come, noble Doctor, 'pray thee let's prevail,
 This is the gentleman, and he is no *Chiaus*.                     30
SUBTLE. Captain, I have returned you all my answer.
 I would do much, sir, for your love—but this
 I neither may, nor can.
FACE.                    Tut, do not say so.
 You deal, now, with a noble fellow, Doctor,
 One that will thank you, richly; and he's no *Chiaus*:            35
 Let that, sir, move you.
SUBTLE.                  Pray you, forbear—
FACE.                              He has

---

1  *Read's matter*  Simon Read, charged with invoking spirits, was pardoned by King James I
   in 1608.
2  *court-hand*  Style of script used in English law courts.
3  *discover*  Reveal (that you broke the law).
4  *Chiaus*  Turkish messenger, referring to an actual incident in 1607 involving a faux ambas-
   sador; proverbial for "cheat."

Four angels,° here—            *gold coins*
SUBTLE.         '       You do me wrong, good sir.
FACE. Doctor, wherein? To tempt you with these spirits?
SUBTLE. To tempt my art, and love, sir, to my peril.
40      Fore heaven, I scarce can think you are my friend,
      That so would draw me to apparent danger.
FACE. I draw you! A horse draw you, and a halter,°   *executioner's noose*
      You, and your flies° together—             *familiar spirits*
DAPPER.             Nay, good Captain.
FACE. That know no difference of men.
SUBTLE.                 Good words, sir.
45 FACE. Good deeds, sir, Doctor dogs-meat. 'Slight, I bring you
      No cheating Clim o' the Cloughs, or Claribels,[1]
      That look as big as five-and-fifty and flush;[2]
      And spit out secrets like hot custard—
DAPPER.             Captain.
FACE. Nor any melancholic under-scribe,
50      Shall tell the Vicar:° but a special gentle,°   *bishop's deputy / gentleman*
      That is the heir to forty marks a year,
      Consorts with the small poets of the time,
      Is the sole hope of his old grandmother,
      That knows the law, and writes you six fair hands,[3]
55      Is a fine clerk, and has his cyph'ring perfect,
      Will take his oath, o' the Greek Xenophon,[4]
      If need be, in his pocket: and can court
      His mistress out of Ovid.[5]
DAPPER.            Nay, dear Captain.
FACE. Did you not tell me so?
DAPPER.            Yes; but I'd ha' you
60      Use master Doctor with some more respect.

---

1  *Clim o' the Cloughs ... Claribels*  Clim o' the Clough was a legendary outlaw; Claribel is a
    knight described as "lewd" in Spenser's *Fairie Queene* (1590–96).
2  *five-and-fifty and flush*  Winning hand in a card game called primero.
3  *six fair hands*  Six styles of handwriting.
4  *Xenophon*  Greek philosopher (c. 430–354 BCE). In the Quarto, this appears as "Testa-
    ment"; it was changed to respect profanity laws, but may also suggest a trick used to swear
    a false oath.
5  *Ovid*  Roman poet (43 BCE–17/18 CE) and author of *The Art of Love.*

FACE. Hang him proud stag, with his broad velvet head.°     *doctor's cap*
    But for your sake, I'd choke, ere I would change°        *exchange*
    An article of breath with such a puck-fist[1]—
    Come, let's be gone.
SUBTLE.              Pray you, le' me speak with you.
DAPPER. His worship calls you, Captain.                 65
FACE.                       I am sorry
    I e'er embarked myself in such a business.
DAPPER. Nay, good sir. He did call you.
FACE.                   Will he take then?
SUBTLE. First, hear me—
FACE. [*He offers money.*]    Not a syllable, 'less you take.
SUBTLE. Pray ye, sir—
FACE.              Upon no terms but an *assumpsit.*[2]
SUBTLE. Your humour must be law.                70
FACE. [*He takes the money.*]     Why now, sir, talk.
    Now I dare hear you with mine honour. Speak.
    So may this gentleman too.
SUBTLE.            Why, sir—

[*Offering to whisper to Face.*]

FACE.                      No whispering.
SUBTLE. 'Fore heaven, you do not apprehend the loss
    You do yourself, in this.
FACE.            Wherein? For what?
SUBTLE. Marry, to be so importunate for one,          75
    That, when he has it, will undo you all:
    He'll win up all the money i' the town.
FACE. How!
SUBTLE.      Yes, and blow up gamester after gamester,
    As they do crackers° in a puppet-play.           *fireworks*
    If I do give him a familiar,                  80
    Give you him all you play for; never set° him:     *bet against*

---

1   *puck-fist*   Puff-ball mushroom; a braggart.
2   *assumpsit*   Voluntary promise, confirmed by an exchange of money.

For he will have it.

FACE.          Y' are mistaken, Doctor.
Why, he does ask one but for cups, and horses,
A rifling fly;[1] none o' your great familiars.

85 DAPPER. Yes, Captain, I would have it for all games.

SUBTLE.  I told you so.

FACE.          'Slight, that is a new business!
I understood you, a tame bird, to fly
Twice in a term, or so; on Friday nights,
When you had left the office, for a nag
90 Of forty, or fifty shillings.

DAPPER.          Ay, 'tis true, sir,
But I do think, now, I shall leave the law,
And therefore—

FACE.          Why, this changes quite the case!
Do you think that I dare move him?

DAPPER.          If you please, sir,
All's one to him, I see.

FACE.          What! For that money?
95 I cannot with my conscience. Nor should you
Make the request, methinks.

DAPPER.          No, sir, I mean
To add consideration.°                    *compensation*

FACE.          Why, then, sir,
I'll try. Say, that it were for all games, Doctor?

SUBTLE.  I say, then, not a mouth shall eat for him
100 At any ordinary, but o' the score,[2]
That is a gaming mouth, conceive me.

FACE.          Indeed!

SUBTLE.  He'll draw you all the treasure of the realm,
If it be set him.

FACE.          Speak you this from art?

SUBTLE.  Ay, sir, and reason too: the ground of art.
105 He's o' the only best complexion,

---

1  *rifling fly* A familiar for playing dice.
2  *not a mouth ... o' the score* No gambler will have money left to buy tavern food except on credit.

The Queen of Fairy loves.

FACE. What! Is he?

SUBTLE. Peace.

He'll overhear you. Sir, should she but see him—

FACE. What?

SUBTLE. Do not you tell him.

FACE. Will he win at cards too?

SUBTLE. The spirits of dead Holland, living Isaac,[1]
  You'd swear were in him: such a vigorous luck          110
  As cannot be resisted. 'Slight, he'll put
  Six o' your gallants to a cloak,[2] indeed.

FACE. A strange success, that some man shall be born to!

SUBTLE. He hears you, man—

DAPPER. Sir, I'll not be ingrateful.

FACE. Faith, I have a confidence in his good nature:        115
  You hear, he says he will not be ingrateful.

SUBTLE. Why, as you please, my venture follows yours.

FACE. Troth, do it, Doctor. Think him trusty, and make him.[3]
  He may make us both happy° in an hour:          *fortunate, rich*
  Win some five thousand pound, and send us two on't.      120

DAPPER. Believe it, and I will, sir.

FACE. And you shall, sir.


(*Face takes him aside.*)


You have heard all?

DAPPER. No, what was't? Nothing, I, sir.

FACE. Nothing?

DAPPER. A little, sir.

FACE. Well, a rare star
  Reign'd, at your birth.

DAPPER. At mine, sir? No.

FACE. The Doctor
  Swears that you are—          125

SUBTLE. Nay, Captain, you'll tell all now.

---

1  *dead Holland, living Isaac*  Dutch alchemists.
2  *Six … to a cloak*  He'll leave six gallants with one cloak among them.
3  *make him*  Make his fortune.

FACE. Ally'd to the Queen of Fairy.
DAPPER.                              Who? That I am?
  Believe it, no such matter—
FACE.                         Yes, and that
  Y' were born with a caul¹ o' your head.
DAPPER.                              Who says so?
FACE.                                       Come,
  You know it well enough, though you dissemble it.
130 DAPPER. I' fac,° I do not. You are mistaken.          *in faith*
FACE.                              How!
  Swear by your fac? And in a thing so known
  Unto the Doctor? How shall we, sir, trust you
  In the other matter? Can we ever think,
  When you have won five, or six thousand pound,
135   You'll send us shares in't, by this rate?
DAPPER.                              By Jove, sir,
  I'll win ten thousand pound, and send you half.
  I' fac's no oath.
SUBTLE.          No, no, he did but jest.
FACE. Go to. Go, thank the Doctor. He's your friend,
  To take it so.
DAPPER.          I thank his worship.
FACE.                              So?
140   Another angel.
DAPPER.          Must I?
FACE.                         Must you? 'Slight,
  What else is thanks? Will you be trivial?° Doctor,          *petty*
  When must he come for his familiar?
DAPPER. Shall I not ha' it with me?²
SUBTLE.                         O, good sir!
  There must a world of ceremonies pass;
145   You must be bath'd and fumigated first;
  Besides the Queen of Fairy does not rise
  Till it be noon.
FACE.          Not if she danc'd, tonight.°          *last night*

---

1  *caul*  Membrane that covers a fetus before birth; when a portion of it still covers a new-
  born's head at birth, it is considered good luck and a safeguard against drowning.
2  *with me*  To bring with me.

SUBTLE.  And she must bless it.
FACE.                         Did you never see
  Her royal Grace yet?
DAPPER.                Whom?
FACE.                    Your aunt¹ of Fairy?
SUBTLE.  Not since she kiss'd him, in the cradle, Captain,          150
  I can resolve you that.
FACE.                  Well, see her Grace,
  Whate'er it cost you, for a thing that I know!
  It will be somewhat hard to compass: but
  How ever, see her. You are made, believe it,
  If you can see her. Her Grace is a lone woman,               155
  And very rich, and if she take a fancy,
  She will do strange things. See her, at any hand.
  'Slid, she may hap to leave you all she has!
  It is the Doctor's fear.
DAPPER.                 How will 't be done, then?
FACE.  Let me alone, take you no thought. Do you          160
  But say to me, Captain, I'll see her Grace.
DAPPER.  Captain, I'll see her Grace.
FACE.                          Enough.

(*One knocks without.*)

SUBTLE.                                  Who's there?
  Anon. (*Aside to Face.*) Conduct him forth by the back way.
  [*To Dapper.*] Sir, against one o'clock, prepare yourself.
  Till when you must be fasting; only, take               165
  Three drops of vinegar in, at your nose,
  Two at your mouth; and one at either ear;
  Then bathe your fingers' ends; and wash your eyes;
  To sharpen your five senses; and cry hum,
  Thrice; and then buzz, as often; and then, come.          170

(*Exit.*)

FACE.  Can you remember this?
DAPPER.                  I warrant you.

---

1  *aunt*  Older female relation, but can also mean "prostitute."

FACE.  Well then, away. 'Tis but your bestowing
    Some twenty nobles,° 'mong Her Grace's servants,        *coins*
    And put on a clean shirt: you do not know
175   What grace her Grace may do you in clean linen.

[*Exeunt Dapper and Face.*]


## ACT I, SCENE 3

SUBTLE.  Come in.

[*Enter Drugger.*]

[*Calls out.*]        Good wives, I pray you forbear me now.
    Troth I can do you no good till afternoon.
    [*To Drugger.*] What is your name, say you, Abel Drugger?
DRUGGER.                         Yes, sir.
SUBTLE.  A seller of tobacco?
DRUGGER.         Yes, sir.
SUBTLE.                   'Umh.
5   Free of the Grocers?[1]
DRUGGER.         Ay, and't please you.
SUBTLE.                  Well—
    Your business, Abel?
DRUGGER.        This, and't please your worship,
    I am a young beginner, and am building
    Of a new shop, and't like your worship, just
    At corner of a street. (Here's the plot° on't.)     *floor plan*
10  And I would know, by art, sir, of your worship,
    Which way I should make my door, by necromancy,
    And where my shelves. And, which should be for boxes.
    And, which for pots. I would be glad to thrive, sir.
    And I was wish'd° to your worship by a gentleman,   *recommended*
15  One Captain Face, that says you know men's planets,[2]
    And their good angels,[3] and their bad.
SUBTLE.               I do,

---

1  *Free of the Grocers*  Full member of the Grocers' guild.
2  *know men's planets*  Can cast men's horoscopes.
3  *angels*  Spirits, punning on coins.

If I do see 'em—

[*Enter Face.*]

FACE.                  What! my honest Abel?
Thou art well met, here!
DRUGGER.                  Troth, sir, I was speaking,
Just as your worship came here, of your worship.
I pray you, speak for me to master Doctor.                    20
FACE.  He shall do anything. Doctor, do you hear?
This is my friend, Abel, an honest fellow,
He lets me have good tobacco, and he does not
Sophisticate it with sack-lees,[1] or oil,
Nor washes it in muscadel,[2] and grains,                     25
Nor buries it in gravel, underground,
Wrapp'd up in greasy leather, or piss'd clouts:[3]
But keeps it in fine lily-pots,[4] that open'd,
Smell like conserve of roses, or French beans.
He has his maple block,[5] his silver tongs,                  30
Winchester pipes, and fire of juniper:[6]
A neat, spruce-honest fellow, and no goldsmith.°    *money-lender*
SUBTLE.  He is a fortunate fellow, that I am sure on—
FACE.  Already, sir, ha' you found it? Lo thee Abel!
SUBTLE.  And in right way toward riches—                      35
FACE.                                    Sir!
SUBTLE.                                    This summer,
He will be of the clothing[7] of his company:
And, next spring, call'd to the scarlet.[8] Spend what he can.
FACE.  What, and so little beard?[9]
SUBTLE.                         Sir, you must think,

---

1  *sack-lees*  Sediment in white wine (sack).
2  *muscadel*  Wine made with muscat grapes.
3  *piss'd clouts*  Pieces of cloth that have been urinated on.
4  *lily-pots*  Flower pots, or decorative jars.
5  *maple block*  Tobacco leaves would be shredded on a block of maple wood.
6  *Winchester pipes*  Famous maker of tobacco pipes;  *fire of juniper*  Long-burning juniper coals were used to light tobacco.
7  *of the clothing*  The livery of the guild.
8  *call'd to the scarlet*  Made sheriff.
9  *so little beard*  So young.

He may have a receipt,° to make hair come:                     *recipe*
40    But he'll be wise, preserve his youth, and fine[1] for 't;
His fortune looks for him another way.
FACE. 'Slid, Doctor, how canst thou know this so soon?
I am amus'd,° at that!                                          *puzzled*
SUBTLE.                     By a rule, Captain,
In metoposcopy,[2] which I do work by,
45    A certain star i' the forehead, which you see not.
Your chestnut, or your olive-colour'd face
Does never fail: and your long ear doth promise.
I knew 't, by certain spots, too, in his teeth,
And on the nail of his mercurial finger.[3]
50  FACE. Which finger's that?
SUBTLE.                     His little finger. Look.
Y' were born upon a Wednesday?
DRUGGER.                          Yes, indeed, sir.
SUBTLE. The thumb, in chiromancy,[4] we give Venus;
The forefinger, to Jove; the midst, to Saturn;
The ring, to Sol; the least, to Mercury,
55    Who was the lord, sir, of his horoscope,
His house of life being Libra, which foreshow'd,
He should be a merchant, and should trade with balance.
FACE. Why, this is strange! Is 't not, honest Nab?
SUBTLE. There is a ship now, coming from Ormus,[5]
60    That shall yield him such a commodity
Of drugs—This is the west, and this the south?

[*Pointing to Drugger's plans.*]

DRUGGER. Yes, sir.
SUBTLE.                     And those are your two sides?
DRUGGER.                                         Ay, sir.
SUBTLE. Make me your door, then, south; your broad side, west:

---

1   *fine*   Pay a fine and refuse the office.
2   *metoposcopy*   Telling a person's fortune by reading the face.
3   *mercurial finger*   The little finger is linked to Mercury, god of businessmen and thieves.
4   *chiromancy*   Palmistry, the telling of fortunes by reading the hand.
5   *Ormus*   Hormuz, a Persian Gulf island, and a rich source in the spice trade.

And, on the east side of your shop, aloft,
Write *Mathlai, Tarmiel,* and *Baraborat;*          65
Upon the north part, *Rael, Velel, Thiel.*[1]
They are the names of those mercurial spirits,
That do fright flies from boxes.[2]

DRUGGER.                                Yes, sir.

SUBTLE.                              And
Beneath your threshold, bury me a loadstone[3]
To draw in gallants that wear spurs. The rest,          70
They'll seem° to follow.                       *be seen*

FACE.                That's a secret, Nab.

SUBTLE. And, on your stall, a puppet with a vice,[4]
· And a court-fucus,° to call city-dames:               *face cosmetic*
You shall deal much, with minerals.

DRUGGER.                         Sir, I have
At home, already—                             75

SUBTLE.              Ay, I know, you've arsenic,
Vitriol, sal-tartar, argaile, alkali,
Cinoper:[5] I know all. This fellow, Captain,
Will come, in time, to be a great distiller,
And give a say[6] (I will not say directly,
But very fair) at the philosopher's stone.          80

FACE. Why, how now, Abel! Is this true?

DRUGGER.                       Good Captain,
What must I give?

FACE.              Nay, I'll not counsel thee.
Thou hear'st what wealth (he says, "Spend what thou canst")
Thou'rt like to come to.

DRUGGER.              I would gi' him a crown.

FACE. A crown! And toward such a fortune? Heart,     85
Thou shalt rather gi' him thy shop. No gold about thee?

---

1  *Mathlai ... Thiel*  Names of angels who guard the east and the north.
2  *fright flies from boxes*  Protect Drugger's stock from insects.
3  *loadstone*  Magnetic oxide of iron (a magnet).
4  *puppet with a vice*  Mechanical doll.
5  *Vitriol, sal-tartar, argaile, alkali, Cinoper*  Sulphuric acid, carbonate of potash, cream of
   tartar, caustic soda, mercuric sulphide, respectively.
6  *give a say*  Make an attempt.

DRUGGER. Yes, I have a portague,[1] I ha' kept this half year.

FACE. Out on thee, Nab; 'Slight, there was such an offer—
'Shalt keep 't no longer, I'll gi 't him for thee?

90     Doctor, Nab prays your worship to drink this: and swears
He will appear more grateful, as your skill
Does raise him in the world.

DRUGGER.                 I would entreat
Another favour of his worship.

FACE.                 What is 't, Nab?

DRUGGER. But to look over, sir, my almanac,[2]

95     And cross out my ill-days,° that I may neither        *unlucky days*
Bargain, nor trust upon them.

FACE.                 That he shall, Nab.
Leave it, it shall be done 'gainst afternoon.

SUBTLE. And a direction for his shelves.

FACE.                   Now, Nab?
Art thou well pleased, Nab?

DRUGGER.         Thank, sir, both your worships.

FACE.                       Away.

[*Exit Drugger.*]

100     Why, now, you smoky persecutor of nature!
Now, do you see, that something's to be done,
Beside your beech-coal,° and your cor'sive° waters,    *charcoal / corrosive*
Your crosslets, crucibles, and cucurbites?[3]
You must have stuff brought home to you, to work on!

105     And yet you think, I am at no expense
In searching out these veins, then following 'em,
Then trying 'em out. 'Fore God, my intelligence°    *information*
Costs me more money, than my share oft comes to,
In these rare works.

SUBTLE.            You're pleasant, sir.—How now?

---

1  *portague*  Portuguese gold coin.
2  *almanac*  Calendar, including astrological and meteorological forecasts.
3  *crosslets, crucibles, and cucurbites*  Alchemical vessels.

# ACT I, SCENE 4

([*Enter*] *Doll*.)

SUBTLE. What says my dainty Dolkin?
DOLL.                              Yonder fishwife
  Will not away. And there's your giantess,
  The bawd of Lambeth.[1]
SUBTLE.                    Heart,[2] I cannot speak with 'em.
DOLL.  Not afore night, I have told 'em in a voice,
  Thorough the trunk,° like one of your familiars.          *speaking tube*  5
  But I have spied sir Epicure Mammon—
SUBTLE.                              Where?
DOLL.  Coming along, at far end of the lane,
  Slow of his feet, but earnest of his tongue,
  To one that's with him.
SUBTLE.                    Face, go you and shift.°          *prepare*

[*Exit Face.*]

  Doll, you must presently° make ready, too.          *immediately*  10
DOLL.  Why, what's the matter?
SUBTLE.                    O, I did look for him
  With the sun's rising: 'marvel he could sleep!
  This is the day I am to perfect for him
  The *magisterium*,[3] our great work, the stone;
  And yield it, made, into his hands: of which          15
  He has, this month, talk'd as he were possess'd.
  And now he's dealing pieces on't away.
  Methinks I see him entering ordinaries,°          *taverns*
  Dispensing for the pox, and plaguy houses,[4]
  Reaching his dose; walking Moorfields[5] for lepers;          20

---

1  *Lambeth*  Disreputable district.
2  *Heart*  Mild oath.
3  *magisterium*  Attainment of the philosopher's stone.
4  *plaguy houses*  Quarantined accommodation for the plague-stricken.
5  *Moorfields*  Suburb occupied by lepers and beggars.

And offering citizens' wives pomander-bracelets,[1]
As his preservative, made of the elixir;
Searching the spittle,[2] to make old bawds young;
And the highways for beggars, to make rich:
25 I see no end of his labours. He will make
Nature asham'd of her long sleep: when art,
Who's but a step-dame, shall do more than she,
In her best love to mankind, ever could:
If his dream lasts, he'll turn the age to gold.


[*Exeunt.*]


## ACT 2, SCENE I

([*Enter*] *Mammon* [*and*] *Surly.*)


MAMMON.   Come on, sir. Now, you set your foot on shore
In *novo orbe*;° here's the rich Peru:[3]                    *new world*
And there within, sir, are the golden mines,
Great Solomon's Ophir![4] He was sailing to 't
5 Three years, but we have reach'd it in ten months.
This is the day, wherein, to all my friends,
I will pronounce the happy word, "be rich."
This day, you shall be *spectatissimi*.°                    *much regarded*
You shall no more deal with the hollow die,°                 *loaded dice*
10 Or the frail° card. No more be at charge of keeping        *unreliable*
The livery-punk,° for the young heir,[5] that must           *pimp*
Seal,[6] at all hours, in his shirt. No more,
If he deny, ha' him beaten to 't, as he is
That brings him the commodity.[7] No more

---

1  *pomander-bracelets*  Perfumed ball carried to protect against the plague.
2  *spittle*  Lazar-house, a charitable hospital for the lower class.
3  *Peru*  Location of the legendary El Dorado and the source of Spanish gold.
4  *Ophir*  Source of King Solomon's gold (see 1 Kings 9.28).
5  *young heir*  Target of a loan swindle.
6  *Seal*  Commit to a fraudulent loan.
7  *commodity*  Part of the loan taken in worthless goods rather than money.

Shall thirst of satin, or the covetous hunger          15
Of velvet entrails° for a rude-spun cloak,                    *lining*
To be display'd at Madam Augusta's,¹ make
The sons of sword and hazard² fall before
The golden calf, and on their knees, whole nights
Commit idolatry with wine and trumpets,             20
Or go a feasting after drum and ensign.°           *rallying cry*
No more of this. You shall start up young Viceroys,
And have your punks, and punketees,° my Surly.    *little prostitutes*
And unto thee, I speak it first, "be rich."
[*Calling.*] Where is my Subtle, there? Within, ho!     25
FACE. (*Within.*)                              Sir,
     He'll come to you by and by.
MAMMON.                          That's his fire-drake,³
His lungs, his Zephyrus,⁴ he that puffs his coals,
Till he firk° nature up, in her own centre.              *stir*
You are not faithful, sir. This night, I'll change
All that is metal in my house, to gold.                30
And, early in the morning, will I send
To all the plumbers and the pewterers,
And buy their tin and lead up; and to Lothbury,⁵
For all the copper.
SURLY.                    What, and turn that too?
MAMMON.  Yes, and I'll purchase Devonshire, and Cornwall,⁶    35
     And make them perfect Indies!⁷ You admire° now?      *wonder*
SURLY.  No, faith.
MAMMON.                But when you see th' effects of the
     great med'cine,°                              *philosopher's stone*
Of which one part projected on a hundred
Of Mercury, or Venus, or the Moon,

---

1  *Madam Augusta*  The madam of a brothel.
2  *sons of sword and hazard*  Adventurers, gamblers.
3  *fire-drake*  Dragon; Mammon associates Face with the dragon as one who blows on fire to
   encourage it, hence his nickname, "Lungs."
4  *Zephyrus*  God of the west wind.
5  *Lothbury*  London street with many coppersmiths.
6  *Devonshire and Cornwall*  English districts with tin and copper mines.
7  *Indies*  Name for India and surrounding regions; it is used symbolically here as a region of
   great wealth.

40    Shall turn it, to as many of the Sun;[1]
       Nay, to a thousand, so *ad infinitum:*°         *to infinity*
       You will believe me.
    SURLY.              Yes, when I see 't, I will.
       But, if my eyes do cozen me so—and I
       Giving 'em no occasion—sure, I'll have
45    A whore, shall piss 'em out next day.
    MAMMON.                 Ha! Why?
       Do you think I fable with you? I assure you,
       He that has once the flower of the sun,
       The perfect ruby, which we call elixir,[2]
       Not only can do that, but by its virtue,
50    Can confer honour, love, respect, long life,
       Give safety, valour: yea, and victory,
       To whom he will. In eight and twenty days,
       I'll make an old man of fourscore, a child.
    SURLY.  No doubt, he's that already.
    MAMMON.               Nay, I mean,
55    Restore his years, renew him like an eagle,
       To the fifth age;[3] make him get sons and daughters,
       Young giants, as our Philosophers have done
       (The ancient Patriarchs, afore the flood)
       But taking, once a week, on a knife's point,
60    The quantity of a grain of mustard of it;
       Become stout Marses[4] and beget young Cupids.
    SURLY.  The decay'd Vestals of Pict-hatch[5] would thank you,
       That keep the fire alive there.
    MAMMON.              'Tis the secret
       Of nature naturized° 'gainst all infections,       *perfected*
65    Cures all diseases coming of all causes,

---

1  *Mercury, or Venus, or the Moon ... Sun*  The stone will turn the various metals associated with the planets (quicksilver, copper, silver) to gold (Sun).

2  *flower of the sun ... perfect ruby ... elixir*  Synonyms for the philosopher's stone. The elixir was a liquid thought to make one immortal.

3  *the fifth age*  According to Renaissance theories, the course of human life was divided into stages, the fifth being maturity.

4  *Marses*  Plural of Mars, Roman god of war.

5  *Vestals of Pict-hatch*  Virgins (sarcastically) of a district of prostitutes (Pict-hatch). Vesta is the chaste Roman goddess of hearth and home, and vestals were traditionally her virgin priestesses.

A month's grief, in a day, a year's, in twelve:
And, of what age soever, in a month,
Past all the doses of your drugging doctors.
I'll undertake, withal, to fright the plague
Out o' the kingdom, in three months.                               70
SURLY.                              And I'll
Be bound, the players shall sing your praises,[1] then,
Without their poets.
MAMMON.                    Sir, I'll do 't. Meantime,
  I'll give away so much unto my man,
  Shall serve th' whole city with preservative,
  Weekly, each house his dose, and at the rate—                     75
SURLY.  As he that built the water-work[2] does with water?
MAMMON.  You are incredulous.
SURLY.                        Faith, I have a humour;
  I would not willingly be gulled.° Your stone           *tricked*
  Cannot transmute me.
MAMMON.                  Pertinax Surly,
  Will you believe antiquity? Records?                             80
  I'll show you a book where Moses and his sister
  And Solomon have written of the art;
  Ay, and a treatise penn'd by Adam—[3]
SURLY.                          How!
MAMMON.  O' the philosopher's stone, and in High Dutch.[4]
SURLY.  Did Adam write, sir, in High Dutch?                        85
MAMMON.                              He did;
  Which proves it was the primitive tongue.
SURLY.                              What paper?
MAMMON.  On cedar board.
SURLY.                  O that, indeed (they say)
  Will last 'gainst worms.
MAMMON.                    'Tis like your Irish wood,[5]

---

1  *players ... praises*  Actors will be happy because the theaters, shut during outbreaks of the
   plague, will remain open.
2  *water-work*  London pumping station.
3  *Moses ... Solomon ... Adam*  Alchemists thought Biblical figures—Moses, Solomon, and
   Adam—were familiar with the mysteries of the philosopher's stone.
4  *High Dutch*  Literary Dutch, thought by some to be the original language.
5  *Irish wood*  Reputed to have been made spider resistant by St. Patrick.

'Gainst cobwebs. I have a piece of Jason's fleece,[1] too,
90  Which was no other than a book of alchemy,
Writ in large sheepskin, a good fat ram-vellum.[2]
Such was Pythagoras'[3] thigh, Pandora's tub,[4]
And all that fable of Medea's[5] charms,
The manner of our work: the bulls, our furnace,
95  Still breathing fire; our *argent-vive*,° the dragon; [6]          quicksilver
The dragon's teeth, mercury sublimate,[7]
That keeps the whiteness, hardness, and the biting;
And they are gathered into Jason's helm,
(Th' alembic[8]) and then sowed in Mars his field,
100 And thence sublimed so often till they are fixed.
Both this, th' Hesperian garden, Cadmus' story,[9]
Jove's shower, the boon of Midas, Argus' eyes,[10]
Boccace his Demogorgon,[11] thousands more,
All abstract riddles° of our stone.                                  *allegories*

([*Enter*] *Face.*)

How now?

---

1   *Jason's fleece*   In Greek mythology, Jason, leader of the Argonauts, took a famous voyage to capture the golden fleece.
2   *ram-vellum*   Fine parchment (a surface for writing) made from the skin of a ram.
3   *Pythogoras*   Pythagoras of Samos (c. 570 BCE) was a Greek mathematician and philosopher.
4   *Pythagoras' thigh*   Reputedly golden; *Pandora's tub*   The box of troubles, according to Greek myth, that was loosed upon the world by the first mortal woman.
5   *Medea*   In Greek mythology, daughter of King Aeëtes of Colchis and niece of the witch Circe. Medea became Jason's wife after helping him capture the Golden Fleece; she was a powerful sorceress.
6   *bulls ... dragon*   Jason's challenges included ploughing a field with two fire-breathing bulls, then battling the warriors that sprang up from the dragon's teeth.
7   *mercury sublimate*   Chloride of mercury.
8   *alembic*   Apparatus for distillation, consisting of two vessels, one for distilling and one for collecting.
9   *Hesperian garden*   Proverbial garden of classical myth, guarded by a dragon; *Cadmus' story*   In Greek mythology, the hero Cadmus was king of Thebes; his slaying of a sacred water-dragon provided the symbolism in alchemy for the slaying of the alchemical dragon (a symbol of renewal).
10  *Jove's shower*   The mythical shower of gold by which Zeus approached Danaë and impregnated her; *Midas*   In Greek mythology, the god Dionysus gave Midas the power of turning all he touched to gold; *Argus' eyes*   Argus is the hundred-eyed giant who guarded the princess Io from Zeus.
11  *Boccace his Demogorgon*   In Boccaccio's *Geneologia Deorum* (*Genealogy of the Gods*), Demogorgon is thought to be the *parentum omnium rerum*, the origin of all things, a parallel to the alchemists' search.

## ACT 2, SCENE 2

MAMMON.  Do we succeed? Is our day come? And holds it?

FACE.  The evening will set red¹ upon you, sir;
   You have colour for it, crimson: the red ferment
   Has done his office. Three hours hence prepare you
   To see projection.                          5

MAMMON.         Pertinax, my Surly.
   Again I say to thee, aloud, "be rich."
   This day, thou shalt have ingots: and tomorrow,
   Give Lords th' affront.² Is it, my Zephyrus, right?
   Blushes the bolt's-head?°                 *alchemical flask*

FACE.                Like a wench with child, sir,
   That were, but now, discovered to her master.          10

MAMMON.  Excellent witty Lungs! My only care is,
   Where to get stuff enough, now, to project on,
   This town will not half serve me.

FACE.               No, sir? Buy
   The coverings off o' churches.³

MAMMON.          That's true.

FACE.               Yes.
   Let 'em stand bare,° as do their auditory.°  *bareheaded | congregation*  15
   Or cap 'em new, with shingles.

MAMMON.         No, good thatch:
   Thatch will lie light upo' the rafters, Lungs.
   Lungs, I will manumit° thee from the furnace;        *free*
   I will restore thee thy complexion, Puff,
   Lost in the embers; and repair this brain,          20
   Hurt wi' the fume o' the metals.

FACE.             I have blown, sir,
   Hard for your worship; thrown by many a coal,
   When 'twas not beech;⁴ weighed those I put in, just,°  *exactly*
   To keep your heat still even; these bleared eyes

---

1  *set red*  Color of the stone in the last stage of the alchemical process. (Note "perfect ruby" at 2.1.48.)

2  *Give ... affront*  Be able to meet lords as equals and even confront them disrespectfully.

3  *coverings off o' churches*  Many churches at the time had lead roofing.

4  *beech*  Charcoal made of beech was thought to produce the steadiest heat.

25  Have waked, to read your several colours,[1] sir,
Of the pale citron, the green lion, the crow,
The peacock's tail, the plumed swan.
MAMMON.                                     And, lastly,
Thou hast descried the flower, the *sanguis agni*?[2]
FACE. Yes, sir.
MAMMON.     Where's master?
FACE.                              At his prayers, sir; he,
30  Good man, he's doing his devotions
For the success.
MAMMON.          Lungs, I will set a period,
To all thy labours: thou shalt be the master
Of my seraglio.°                                    *harem*
FACE.          Good, sir.
MAMMON.                    But do you hear?
I'll geld you, Lungs.
FACE.          Yes, sir.
MAMMON.              For I do mean
35  To have a list of wives and concubines,
Equal with Solomon;[3] who had the stone
Alike, with me; and I will make me a back
With the elixir, that shall be as tough
As Hercules,[4] to encounter fifty a night.
40  Th' art sure thou saw'st it blood?
FACE.                    Both blood, and spirit, sir.
MAMMON. I will have all my beds, blown up; not stuffed:
Down is too hard. And then, mine oval room,
Filled with such pictures as Tiberius took

---

1   *colours*  Colors of the alchemical "path" or process, represented by animals and birds (lion, crow, peacock, swan).
2   *sanguis agni*  Latin, for "blood of the lamb." It is red, like the stone in its last stage, and its connection to Christ is another link to immortality.
3   *Solomon*  The Hebrew king was said to have had seven hundred wives and three hundred concubines (I *Kings* 11.3).
4   *Hercules*  The Greek hero was said to have impregnated the fifty daughters of King Thespius in one night.

From Elephantis,[1] and dull Aretine[2]
But coldly imitated. Then, my glasses,°        *mirrors*    45
Cut in more subtle angles, to disperse
And multiply the figures, as I walk
Naked between my *succubae*. My mists[3]
I'll have of perfume, vapoured 'bout the room,
To lose ourselves in; and my baths, like pits        50
To fall into; from whence we will come forth,
And roll us dry in gossamer[4] and roses.
(Is it arrived at ruby?)—Where I spy
A wealthy citizen, or rich lawyer,
Have a sublimed pure wife, unto that fellow        55
I'll send a thousand pound to be my cuckold.
FACE.  And I shall carry it?
MAMMON.                    No. I'll ha' no bawds,
But fathers and mothers. They will do it best,
Best of all others. And my flatterers
Shall be the pure and gravest of divines        60
That I can get for money. My mere fools,
Eloquent burgesses,° and then my poets        *townspeople*
The same that writ so subtly of the fart,[5]
Whom I will entertain still for that subject.
The few that would give out themselves to be        65
Court and town stallions, and, each where, belie°        *slander*
Ladies, who are known most innocent, for them;
Those will I beg to make me eunuchs of:
And they shall fan me with ten ostrich tails
Apiece, made in a plume, to gather wind.        70

---

1  *Tiberius took ... Elephantis*  Roman Emperor Tiberius (14 BCE–37 CE) had an orgy room at
   his villa at Capri, which was described by Suetonius as being decorated with erotic pictures
   taken from the writings of Elephantis.
2  *Aretine*  Pietro Aretino (1492–1556), Italian poet, whose erotic *Sonnetti Lussuriosi* (1524)
   were illustrated by Giulio Romano.
3  *succubae*  Female demons that would have intercourse with sleeping men;  *mists*  An
   allusion to the Roman Emperor Nero's (37–68) palace that, according to Suetonius, sprayed
   perfumed oils on guests.
4  *gossamer*  Light, filmy substance; silk.
5  *fart*  Refers to a recent 1607 parliamentary incident involving one member's farting in
   response to another's argument, commemorated by many poets, including Jonson.

We will be brave, Puff, now we ha' the med'cine.
My meat shall all come in, in Indian shells,
Dishes of agate, set in gold, and studded,
With emeralds, sapphires, hyacinths,[1] and rubies.
75    The tongues of carps, dormice, and camels' heels,[2]
Boiled i' the spirit of Sol,° and dissolved pearl,[3]          *distilled gold*
(Apicius'[4] diet, 'gainst the epilepsy)
And I will eat these broths with spoons of amber,
Headed with diamond and carbuncle.
80    My foot-boy shall eat pheasants, calvered[5] salmons,
Knots, godwits, lampreys:[6] I myself will have
The beards of barbels° served instead of salads;          *carp-like fish*
Oiled mushrooms; and the swelling unctuous paps°          *udders*
Of a fat pregnant sow, newly cut off,
85    Dressed with an exquisite and poignant sauce;
For which I'll say unto my cook, "There's gold,
Go forth, and be a knight."[7]
FACE.                    Sir, I'll go look
A little, how it heightens.
MAMMON.                    Do.

[*Exit Face.*]

                         My shirts
I'll have of taffeta-sarsnet,° soft and light          *fine silk*
90    As cobwebs; and for all my other raiment,
It shall be such as might provoke the Persian,[8]
Were he to teach the world riot anew.
My gloves of fishes' and birds' skins, perfumed

---

1  *hyacinths*  Precious blue stones.
2  *dormice, and camels' heels*  Roman delicacies.
3  *dissolved pearl*  Cleopatra (69–30 BCE) is said to have drunk a pearl dissolved in vinegar. Cf. *Volpone* 3.7.191–93.
4  *Apicius*  Marcus Gavius Apicius, a Roman living during the reign of Tiberius; he was a famous glutton and epicure. A book of Roman recipes is named for him.
5  *calvered*  Sliced while alive (or very fresh) and pickled.
6  *Knots*  Long-billed game birds;  *godwits*  Marsh birds;  *lampreys*  Eel-like fish.
7  *be a knight*  A dig at the practice under James I of granting knighthoods for a fee. Jonson was imprisoned in 1605 for satirizing this practice in *Eastward Ho!*
8  *Persian*  Proverbial for luxury.

With gums of paradise[1] and eastern air—
SURLY. And do you think to have the stone, with this?                  95
MAMMON. No, I do think t' have all this, with the stone.
SURLY. Why, I have heard he must be *homo frugi*,[2]
  A pious, holy, and religious man,
  One free from mortal sin, a very virgin.
MAMMON. That makes it, sir, he is so. But I buy it.                  100
  My venture brings it me. He, honest wretch,
  A notable, superstitious, good soul,
  Has worn his knees bare, and his slippers bald,
  With prayer and fasting for it: and, sir, let him
  Do it alone for me, still. Here he comes.                  105
  Not a profane word afore him: 'tis poison.


## ACT 2, SCENE 3

([*Enter*] *Subtle*.)

MAMMON. Good morrow, father.
SUBTLE.                   Gentle son, good morrow.
  And to your friend, there. What is he is with you?
MAMMON. An heretic, that I did bring along,
  In hope, sir, to convert him.
SUBTLE.              Son, I doubt°        *suspect*
  Y' are covetous, that thus you meet your time                  5
  I' the just point:[3] prevent° your day, at morning.    *anticipate*
  This argues something, worthy of a fear
  Of importune,° and carnal appetite.            *urgent*
  Take heed you do not cause the blessing leave you,
  With your ungoverned haste. I should be sorry,                  10
  To see my labours, now e'en at perfection,
  Got by long watching and large patience,
  Not prosper, where my love and zeal hath placed 'em—
  Which (heaven I call to witness, with yourself,
  To whom I have poured my thoughts) in all my ends,                  15

---

1  *gums of paradise*  Incense from Eden, thought to have been located in the Middle East.
2  *homo frugi*  Latin: a temperate man. Piety and restraint were thought to be prerequisites for
  success in alchemy.
3  *I' the just point*  At exactly the right time; punctually.

Have looked no way, but unto public good,
To pious uses, and dear charity,
Now grown a prodigy° with men. Wherein          *rare event*
If you, my son, should now prevaricate,°          *deceive*
20  And, to your own particular lusts employ
So great and catholic° a bliss, be sure,          *universal*
A curse will follow, yea, and overtake
Your subtle and most secret ways.
MAMMON.                                    I know, sir;
You shall not need to fear me. I but come,
25  To ha' you confute this gentleman.
SURLY.                                    Who is,
Indeed, sir, somewhat costive° of belief          *slow*
Toward your stone: would not be gulled.
SUBTLE.                                    Well, son,
All that I can convince him in is this,
The work is done: bright *Sol* is in his robe.¹
30  We have a med'cine of the triple soul,²
The glorified spirit. Thanks be to heaven,
And make us worthy of it. [*Calling.*] Ulen Spiegel!³


[*Enter Face.*]


FACE. Anon, sir.
SUBTLE.            Look well to the register.⁴
And let your heat still lessen by degrees,
35  To the aludels.⁵
FACE.            Yes, sir.
SUBTLE.                        Did you look

---

1  *bright Sol is in his robe*  Sol, the sun, the planet of gold, is in his robe, like a king or a judge,
   ready to officiate.
2  *triple soul*  The human soul was thought to have a tripartite makeup, of vital, natural, and
   animal spirits.
3  *Ulen Spiegel*  Til Owlglass, a trickster in German folklore.
4  *register*  Metal plate or other device used to regulate the heat of a fireplace or furnace.
5  *aludels*  Stackable, pear-shaped earthenware pots used in sublimation.

O' the bolt's-head yet?
FACE. Which? On D¹ sir?
SUBTLE. Ay.
What's the complexion?
FACE. Whitish.
SUBTLE. Infuse vinegar,
To draw his volatile substance, and his tincture:
And let the water in Glass E be filtered,
And put into the gripe's egg.² Lute° him well;                    *seal* 40
And leave him closed in *balneo*.°                    *bath*
FACE. I will, sir.


[*Exit Face.*]


SURLY. What a brave language here is, next to canting!°    *thieves' jargon*
SUBTLE. I've another work you never saw, son,
That three days since, passed the philosopher's wheel,³
In the lent heat of athanor;⁴ and's become                    45
Sulphur o' nature.°                    *pure sulphur*
MAMMON. But 'tis for me?
SUBTLE. What need you?
You have enough, in that is perfect.
MAMMON. O but—
SUBTLE. Why, this is covetise!⁵
MAMMON. No, I assure you,
I shall employ it all in pious uses,
Founding of colleges, and grammar schools,                    50
Marrying⁶ young virgins, building hospitals,

---

1 *On D*   D, and the following lettered references, refer to various alchemical projects Subtle supposedly has in the works.
2 *gripe's egg*   Alchemical vessel shaped like a vulture's (gripe's) egg.
3 *philosopher's wheel*   An auspicious point in the alchemical process.
4 *lent heat of athanor*   Slow burning furnace that retains heat.
5 *covetise*   Covetousness, or greed, an ill-advised moral posture for one in search of the philosopher's stone.
6 *Marrying*   Giving dowries for.

And now and then, a church.

([*Enter*] *Face.*)

SUBTLE.                     How now?
FACE.                            Sir, please you,
  Shall I not change the filter?
SUBTLE.                     Marry, yes,
  And bring me the complexion of Glass B.

[*Exit Face.*]

55 MAMMON. Ha' you another?
SUBTLE.                 Yes, son, were I assur'd
  Your piety were firm, we would not want
  The means to glorify° it. But I hope the best.      *refine*
  I mean to tinct C in sand-heat[1] tomorrow,
  And give him imbibition.°                 *steeping*
MAMMON.             Of white oil?
60 SUBTLE. No, sir, of red. F is come over the helm too,
  I thank my Maker, in St. Mary's bath,[2]
  And shows *lac Virginis.*[3] Blessed be heaven.
  I sent you of his faeces° there, calcin'd.[4]    *sediment*
  Out of that calx° I ha' won the salt of mercury.[5]   *powder*
65 MAMMON. By pouring on your rectified° water?   *distilled*
SUBTLE. Yes, and reverberating in athanor.

[*Enter Face.*]

How now? What colour says it?
FACE.                 The ground black, sir.

---

1  *sand-heat*  Method of heating in a bath of hot sand.
2  *St. Mary's bath*  Also known as a bain-marie: a double-boiler.
3  *lac Virginis*  Latin: virgin's milk; dissolved mercury.
4  *calcin'd*  Rendered to powder by burning.
5  *salt of mercury*  Mercury oxide.

MAMMON. That's your crow's head?[1]

SURLY.                             Your cock's-comb's,[2] is 't not?

SUBTLE. No, 'tis not perfect, would it were the crow.
  That work wants something.                                                70

SURLY. (*Aside.*)              O, I look'd for this.
  The hay is a-pitching.[3]

SUBTLE.              Are you sure you loosed° 'em              *dissolved*
  In their own menstrue?°                                      *solvent*

FACE.              Yes, sir, and then married° 'em,   *combined*
  And put 'em in a bolt's-head, nipped° to digestion,[4]        *sealed*
  According as you bade me; when I set
  The liquor of Mars° to circulation,              *molten iron*   75
  In the same heat.

SUBTLE.     ⸻        The process, then, was right.

FACE. Yes, by the token, sir; the retort brake,
  And what was saved was put into the pelican,[5]
  And signed with Hermes' seal.[6]

SUBTLE.              I think 'twas so.
  We should have a new amalgama.[7]                               80

SURLY. (*Aside.*)              O, this ferret
  Is rank as any polecat.[8]

SUBTLE.              But I care not.
  Let him e'en die; we have enough beside
  In *embrion*.° H has his white shirt on?[9]         *beginning stage*

FACE.              Yes, sir,
  He's ripe for inceration:[10] he stands warm,
  In his ash-fire. I would not, you should let                   85
  Any die now, if I might counsel, sir,

---

1  *crow's head*   Black ash resulting from calcination.
2  *cock's-comb's*   A coxcomb is a conceited and pretentious fool.
3  *hay is a-pitching*   A net ("hay") is being set ("pitched") to catch rabbits.
4  *digestion*   Extraction of soluble substances by cooking in a "digestive" oven.
5  *pelican*   Long-necked alchemical vessel.
6  *Hermes' seal*   Hermetically sealed.
7  *amalgama*   Mixture of metals and mercury.
8  *ferret ... polecat*   Ferrets were placed in rabbits' burrows to flush them out into the nets;
   Surly is continuing his earlier analogy. Polecats, a small carnivorous animal found in
   Europe, are known for being smelly (rank).
9  *has his white shirt on*   Has turned white.
10  *inceration*   Covering in wax; made wax-like.

For luck's sake to the rest. It is not good.

MAMMON.  He says right.

SURLY.  [*Aside.*]            Ay, are you bolted?°            *trapped*

FACE.                                       Nay, I know 't, sir,
   I have seen th' ill fortune. What is some three ounces
90   Of fresh materials?

MAMMON.            Is't no more?

FACE.                         No more, sir.
   Of gold, t'amalgam with some six of mercury.

MAMMON.  Away, here's money. What will serve?

FACE.                               Ask him, sir.

MAMMON.  How much?

SUBTLE.            Give him nine pound: you may gi' him ten.

SURLY.  (*Aside.*)  Yes, twenty, and be cozened, do.

MAMMON.                               There 'tis.

95 SUBTLE.  This needs not. But that you will have it, so,
   To see conclusions of all. For two
   Of our inferior works are at fixation.
   A third is in ascension.¹ Go your ways.
   Ha' you set the oil of *Luna* in *kemia*?²

100 FACE.  Yes, sir.

SUBTLE.      And the philosopher's vinegar?³

FACE.                               Ay.


   [*Exit.*]


SURLY.  [*Aside.*] We shall have a salad.

MAMMON.                    When do you make projection?

SUBTLE.  Son, be not hasty, I exalt our med'cine,
   By hanging him in *balneo vaporoso*,°            *steam bath*
   And giving him solution;° then congeal him;            *dissolution*
105   And then dissolve him; then again congeal him;
   For look, how oft I iterate the work,
   So many times I add unto his virtue.

---

1   *For two … ascension*  Dapper and Drugger are the "inferior works," both "fixed' or stable.
    Mammon is the "third" who is in ascension, still in the process of being refined, i.e., duped.
2   *oil of Luna in kemia*  "White elixir" in a "kemia" vessel, used for chemical analysis.
3   *philosopher's vinegar*  Corrosive liquid used to dissolve metals.

As, if at first one ounce convert a hundred,
After his second loose,° he'll turn a thousand;   *solution*
His third solution, ten; his fourth, a hundred;    110
After his fifth, a thousand thousand ounces
Of any imperfect metal, into pure
Silver, or gold, in all examinations,
As good as any of the natural mine.
Get you your stuff here, against afternoon,     115
Your brass, your pewter, and your andirons.[1]

MAMMON. Not those of iron?

SUBTLE.       Yes, you may bring them, too:
We'll change all metals.

SURLY. [*Aside.*]    I believe you in that.

MAMMON. Then I may send my spits?[2]

SUBTLE.        Yes, and your racks.

SURLY. And dripping-pans, and pot-hangers, and hooks,   120
Shall he not?

SUBTLE.   If he please.

SURLY.     To be an ass.

SUBTLE. How, sir!

MAMMON.   This gentleman you must bear withal.
I told you, he had no faith.

SURLY.      And little hope, sir,
But much less charity,[3] should I gull myself.

SUBTLE. Why, what have you observed, sir, in our art,   125
Seems so impossible?

SURLY.     But your whole work, no more.
That you should hatch gold in a furnace, sir,
As they do eggs, in Egypt![4]

SUBTLE.     Sir, do you
Believe that eggs are hatch'd so?

SURLY.     If I should?

SUBTLE. Why, I think that the greater miracle.    130
No egg but differs from a chicken more

---

1 *andirons* Iron supports for wood in a fireplace.
2 *spits* Long, thin cooking implements for spearing meat.
3 *faith ... charity* Cf. 1 Corinthians 13.13.
4 *eggs, in Egypt* Egyptians were known to hatch eggs using incubators.

Than metals in themselves.

SURLY.                          That cannot be.

The egg's ordained by nature, to that end,

And is a chicken *in potentia*.°                          *potential*

135  SUBTLE.  The same we say of lead, and other metals,

Which would be gold, if they had time.

MAMMON.                          And that

Our art doth further.

SUBTLE.                          Ay, for 'twere absurd

To think that nature in the earth bred gold

Perfect, i' the instant. Something went before.

140  There must be remote matter.

SURLY.                          Ay, what is that?

SUBTLE.  Marry, we say—

MAMMON.                          Ay, now it heats: stand, father,

Pound him to dust—

SUBTLE.                          It is, of the one part,

A humid exhalation, which we call

*Materia liquida*,° or the unctuous water;                          *liquid matter*

145  On th' other part, a certain crass and viscous

Portion of earth; both which, concorporate,°                          *united*

Do make the elementary matter of gold:

Which is not, yet, *propria materia*,°                          *particular substance*

But common to all metals and all stones.

150  For, where it is forsaken of that moisture,

And hath more dryness, it becomes a stone;

Where it retains more of the humid fatness,[1]

It turns to sulphur, or to quicksilver,

Who are the parents of all other metals.[2]

155  Nor can this remote matter, suddenly

Progress so from extreme unto extreme,

As to grow gold, and leap o'er all the means.°                          *intermediate stages*

Nature doth first beget th' imperfect; then

Proceeds she to the perfect. Of that airy,

---

1  *humid fatness*  Metals were thought to have a predominance of moist qualities, making them fusible and malleable (unlike stone).

2  *parents of all other metals*  Sulphur and mercury were thought to be the components of all other metals.

And oily water, mercury is engendered;                                        160
Sulphur o' the fat and earthy part: the one,
Which is the last, supplying the place of male,
The other of the female, in all metals.
Some do believe hermaphrodeity,[1]
That both do act, and suffer.[2] But these two                                165
Make the rest ductile, malleable, extensive.[3]
And, even in gold, they are; for we do find
Seeds of them, by our fire, and gold in them:
And can produce the species of each metal
More perfect thence, than nature doth in earth.                               170
Beside, who doth not see, in daily practice,
Art can beget bees, hornets, beetles, wasps,
Out of the carcasses, and dung of creatures;[4]
Yea, scorpions, of an herb, being rightly placed:
And these are living creatures, far more perfect                              175
And excellent, than metals.
MAMMON.                         Well said, father!
    Nay, if he take you in hand, sir, with an argument,
    He'll bray° you in a mortar.                                    *pound*
SURLY.                         Pray you, sir, stay.
    Rather than I'll be brayed, sir, I'll believe
    That alchemy is a pretty kind of game,                                    180
    Somewhat like tricks o' the cards, to cheat a man
    With charming.
SUBTLE.           Sir?
SURLY.                    What else are all your terms,
    Whereon no one o' your writers 'grees with other?
    Of your elixir, your *lac Virginis*,
    Your stone, your med'cine, and your chrysosperm,°        *seed of gold* 185
    Your sal,° your sulphur, and your mercury,                        *salt*

---

1   *hermaphrodeity*  Being a hermaphrodite. In alchemy, chemical reactions were variously
    described as marriages, as copulations, or as combining male and female opposites into a
    hermaphrodite.
2   *do act, and suffer*  Are active and passive.
3   *extensive*  Capable of being extended.
4   *Art can beget bees ... dung of creatures*  It was mistakenly thought that insects were generated
    spontaneously from dead bodies and dung.

Your oil of height, your tree of life, your blood, [1]
Your marcasite, your tutty, your magnesia, [2]
Your toad, your crow, your dragon, and your panther; [3]
190    Your sun, your moon, your firmament, your adrop,°      *lead*
Your lato, azoch, zernich, chibrit, heautarit, [4]
And then, your red man, and your white woman, [5]
With all your broths, your menstrues, and materials,
Of piss, and egg-shells, women's terms, [6] man's blood,
195    Hair o' the head, burnt clouts, chalk, merds,° and clay,     *faeces*
Powder of bones, scalings of iron, glass,
And worlds of other strange ingredients,
Would burst a man to name?
SUBTLE.                 And all these, named,
Intending but one thing; which art our writers
200    Used to obscure their art.
MAMMON.             Sir, so I told him,
Because the simple idiot should not learn it,
And make it vulgar.
SUBTLE.           Was not all the knowledge
Of the Egyptians writ in mystic symbols?
Speak not the Scriptures, oft, in parables?
205    Are not the choicest fables of the poets,
That were the fountains and first springs of wisdom,
Wrapped in perplexed allegories?
MAMMON.               I urg'd that,
And cleared to him that Sisyphus was damn'd
To roll the ceaseless stone, [7] only because

---

1   *oil of height* Prime salt;   *tree of life* Alchemical diagram;   *blood* Red color of successful alchemical completion.
2   *marcasite* Iron pyrite;   *tutty* Impure zinc oxide;   *magnesia* Thick salty water.
3   *Your toad ... your panther* Colors (represented by animals) at various stages of the alchemical process.
4   *lato* Latten, a metal similar to brass;   *azoch* Mercury;   *zernich* Trisulphide of arsenic;   *chibrit* Sulphur;   *heautarit* Mercury.
5   *red man* Sulphur;   *white woman* Mercury.
6   *women's terms* Menstrual blood.
7   *Sisyphus ... ceaseless stone* In Greek mythology, Sisyphus was condemned to roll a large stone up a hill, only to have it roll down again, for eternity. It was punishment for being overly crafty and ambitious.

He would have made ours common.                          210

(*Doll is seen.*)

                                        Who is this?
SUBTLE.  God's precious—What do you mean? Go in, good lady,
Let me entreat you.

[*Exit Doll.*]

                      Where's this varlet?

[*Enter Face.*]

FACE.                                        Sir?
SUBTLE.  You very knave! Do you use me thus?
FACE.                                        Wherein, sir?
SUBTLE.  Go in, and see, you traitor. Go.

[*Exit Face.*]

MAMMON.                              Who is it, sir?
SUBTLE.  Nothing, sir. Nothing.                          215
MAMMON.                    What's the matter? Good sir!
I have not seen you thus distempered. Who is 't?
SUBTLE.  All arts have still had, sir, their adversaries,
But ours the most ignorant.

(*Face returns.*)

                      What now?
FACE.  'Twas not my fault, sir, she would speak with you.
SUBTLE.  Would she, sir? Follow me.                      220

[*Exit.*]

MAMMON.                              Stay, Lungs.
FACE.                                        I dare not, sir.

MAMMON.  How! Pray thee stay.

FACE.                                      She's mad, sir, and sent hither—

MAMMON.  Stay man, what is she?

FACE.                                      A lord's sister, sir.
  He'll be mad too—

MAMMON.                  I warrant° thee. Why sent hither?               *assure*

FACE.  Sir, to be cured.

SUBTLE.  [*Within.*]      Why, rascal!

FACE.                                      Lo, you. [*Calling.*] Here, sir!


(*He goes out.*)

225  MAMMON.  'Fore-God, a Bradamante,[1] a brave piece.°               *woman*

SURLY.  Heart, this is a bawdy-house!° I'll be burnt else.               *brothel*

MAMMON.  O, by this light, no. Do not wrong him. He's
  Too scrupulous, that way. It is his vice.
  No, he's a rare physician, do him right.

230  An excellent Paracelsian![2] And has done
  Strange cures with mineral physic. He deals all
  With spirits, he. He will not hear a word
  Of Galen,[3] or his tedious recipes.


([*Enter*] *Face again.*)

  How now, Lungs!

FACE.                  Softly, sir, speak softly. I meant

235  To ha' told your worship all. This° must not hear.               *Surly*

MAMMON.  No, he will not be gulled; let him alone.

FACE.  Y'are very right, sir. She is a most rare scholar:
  And is gone mad, with studying Broughton's[4] works.
  If you but name a word, touching the Hebrew,

240  She falls into her fit, and will discourse
  So learnedly of genealogies,

---

1  *Bradamante*  Female knight in Ariosto's *Orlando Furioso*.
2  *Paracelsian*  Follower of Paracelsus (1493–1541), Swiss physician and alchemist who first
   applied chemistry to the study of medicine.
3  *Galen*  Second-century Roman physician and medieval authority on medicine.
4  *Broughton*  Hugh Broughton (1549–1612), English scholar and rabbinical theologian.

As you would run mad, too, to hear her, sir.
MAMMON. How might one do t' have conference with her, Lungs?
FACE. O, divers have run mad upon the conference.
    I do not know, sir: I am sent in haste,     245
    To fetch a vial.
SURLY.           Be not gulled, Sir Mammon.
MAMMON. Wherein? Pray ye, be patient.
SURLY.                     Yes, as you are.
    And trust confederate knaves, and bawds, and whores.
MAMMON. You are too foul, believe it. Come here, Ulen,[1]
    One word.     250
FACE.       I dare not, in good faith.
MAMMON.               Stay, knave.
FACE. He's extreme angry, that you saw her, sir.
MAMMON. Drink that. [*Gives him money.*] What is she when she's
    out of her fit?
FACE. O, the most affablest creature, sir! So merry!
    So pleasant! She'll mount you up, like quicksilver,
    Over the helm; and circulate like oil,     255
    A very vegetal:[2] discourse of state,
    Of mathematics, bawdry, anything—
MAMMON. Is she no way accessible? No means,
    No trick to give a man a taste of her—wit—
    Or so? Ulen.[3]     260
FACE.          I'll come to you again, sir.

[*Exit.*]

MAMMON. Surly, I did not think one o' your breeding
    Would traduce personages of worth.
SURLY.                Sir Epicure,
    Your friend to use: yet, still, loth to be gulled.
    I do not like your philosophical bawds.

---

1  *Ulen*  Zephyrus, God of the west wind (one of Mammon's nicknames for Face).
2  *vegetal*  According to Aristotle, the lowest level of soul is the vegetal, which has to do with growth and reproduction.
3  *Ulen*  Omitted in the 1612 Quarto. While it is included in the Folio as part of Mammon's speech, it may be spoken by Subtle from within, prompting Face's departure.

265 Their stone is lechery enough to pay for,
    Without this bait.
    MAMMON.            Heart, you abuse yourself.
    I know the lady, and her friends, and means,
    The original° of this disaster. Her brother           *cause*
    Has told me all.
    SURLY.            And yet, you ne'er saw her
270 Till now?
    MAMMON.     O yes, but I forgot. I have (believe it)
    One o' the treacherous'st memories, I do think,
    Of all mankind.
    SURLY.          What call you her brother?
    MAMMON.                  My lord—
    He wi' not have his name known, now I think on't.
    SURLY. A very treacherous memory!
    MAMMON.               O' my faith—
275 SURLY. Tut, if you ha' it not about you, pass it,
    Till we meet next.
    MAMMON.         Nay, by this hand, 'tis true.
    He's one I honour, and my noble friend,
    And I respect his house.
    SURLY.            Heart! Can it be,
    That a grave sir, a rich, that has no need,
280 A wise sir, too, at other times, should thus,
    With his own oaths and arguments, make hard means
    To gull himself? And this be your elixir,
    Your *lapis mineralis*, and your lunary,[1]
    Give me your honest trick, yet, at primero,
285 Or gleek;[2] and take your *lutum sapientis*,[3]
    Your *menstruum simplex*![4] I'll have gold before you,
    And with less danger of the quicksilver;

---

1  *lapis mineralis*  Mineral stone, another name for the philosopher's stone;  *lunary*  Moon-wort, a plant, also called honesty.
2  *primero*  Spanish card game;  *gleek*  Card game.
3  *lutum sapientis*  Paste used to seal alchemical vessels.
4  *menstruum simplex*  Simple solvent.

Or the hot sulphur.[1]

[*Re-enter Face.*]

FACE. (*To Surly.*)        Here's one from Captain Face, sir,
Desires you meet him i' the Temple church,[2]
Some half hour hence, and upon earnest business.                    290

(*He whispers Mammon.*)

Sir, if you please to quit us, now, and come
Again within two hours, you shall have
My master busy examining o' the works;
And I will steal you in, unto the party,
That you may see her converse. (*To Surly.*) Sir, shall I say,      295
You'll meet the Captain's worship?
SURLY.                              Sir, I will.
[*Aside.*] But by attorney, and to a second purpose.
Now, I am sure, it is a bawdy-house;
I'll swear it, were the marshal here, to thank me:
The naming this commander doth confirm it.                          300
Don Face! Why he's the most authentic dealer
I' these commodities! The superintendant
To all the quainter traffickers[3] in town.
He is their visitor° and does appoint                    inspector
Who lies with whom, and at what hour, what price,                   305
Which gown, and in what smock, what fall, what tire.[4]
Him will I prove,° by a third person, to find              test
The subtleties of this dark labyrinth:
Which, if I do discover, dear Sir Mammon,
You'll give your poor friend leave, though no philosopher,          310
To laugh: for you that are, 'tis thought, shall weep.
FACE. Sir, he does pray you'll not forget.
SURLY.                              I will not, sir.

---

1   *quicksilver … hot sulphur* Mercury (quicksilver) was used to treat sexually transmitted
    infections, particularly syphilis. Sulphur, similarly, was used to treat skin infections.
2   *Temple church* Church for law students; a common meeting place for lawyers and clients.
3   *quainter* Pun on "quaint" and "cunt"; *traffickers* Pimps.
4   *fall* Flat collar; *tire* Headdress.

Sir Epicure, I shall leave you.

[*Exit.*]

MAMMON.                    I follow you straight.
FACE.  But do so, good sir, to avoid suspicion.
315  This gentleman has a parlous° head.                    *cunning*
MAMMON.                    But wilt thou, Ulen,
    Be constant to thy promise?
FACE.                    As my life, sir.
MAMMON.  And wilt thou insinuate what I am? And praise me?
    And say I am a noble fellow?
FACE.                    Oh, what else, sir?
    And—that you'll make her royal with the stone,
320  An empress; and yourself, King of Bantam.[1]
MAMMON.  Wilt thou do this?
FACE.                    Will I, sir?
MAMMON.                    Lungs, my Lungs!
    I love thee.
FACE.          Send your stuff, sir, that my master
    May busy himself, about projection.
MAMMON.  Th' hast witched me, rogue. [*He gives him money.*]
    Take, go.
FACE.          Your jack,[2] and all, sir.
325  MAMMON.  Thou art a villain—I will send my jack;
    And the weights too. Slave, I could bite thine ear.[3]
    Away, thou dost not care for me.
FACE.                    Not I, sir?
MAMMON.  Come, I was born to make thee, my good weasel;
    Set thee on a bench: and ha' thee twirl a chain
330  With the best lord's vermin[4] of 'em all.
FACE.                    Away, sir.

---

1  *Bantam*  Indonesia (Java), reputed for wealth.
2  *jack*  Machine driven by weights, used to turn a spit.
3  *bite thine ear*  Affectionate gesture.
4  *vermin*  Pun on "vermin" and "ermine." The ermine is a member of the weasel family, and its fur was used to line the cloaks of judges.

MAMMON.  A Count, nay, a Count Palatine—¹
FACE.                                    Good, sir, go.
MAMMON.  Shall not advance thee better: no, nor faster.

[*Exit Mammon.*]

## ACT 2, SCENE 4

([*Enter*] *Subtle* [*and*] *Doll.*)

SUBTLE.  Has he bit? Has he bit?
FACE.                            And swallowed, too, my Subtle.
    I ha' giv'n him line, and now he plays, i' faith.
SUBTLE.  And shall we twitch him?
FACE.                            Thorough both the gills.
    A wench is a rare bait, with which a man
    No sooner's taken, but he straight firks² mad.                         5
SUBTLE.  Doll, my Lord What's-um's sister, you must now
    Bear yourself *statelich.*°                              *stately*
DOLL.                    Oh let me alone.
    I'll not forget my race,° I warrant you.                *breeding*
    I'll keep my distance, laugh, and talk aloud;
    Have all the tricks of a proud scurvy° lady,         *worthless*  10
    And be as rude as her woman.
FACE.                    Well said, Sanguine.³
SUBTLE.  But will he send his andirons?
FACE.                            His jack too;
    And's iron shoeing-horn: I ha' spoke to him. Well,
    I must not lose my wary gamester, yonder.
SUBTLE.  Oh Monsieur Caution, that will not be gulled?                     15
FACE.                                    Aye,
    If I can strike a fine hook into him, now—
    The Temple-church, there I have cast mine angle.

---

1   *Count Palatine*   Count with king-like authority over his region.
2   *firks*   Thrashes about.
3   *Sanguine*   Face is identifying Doll as one of "sanguine" temperament: brave, optimistic,
    and amorous.

Well, pray for me. I'll about it.

(*One knocks.*)

SUBTLE.                                                     What, more gudgeons!°          *gulls*
Doll, scout, scout.
                                        Stay, Face, you must go to the door.
20      Pray God it be my Anabaptist.¹ Who is't, Doll?
DOLL.  I know him not: he looks like a gold-end man.²
SUBTLE.  Gods so! 'Tis he, he said he would send. What call you
        him?
The sanctified elder, that should deal
For Mammon's jack, and andirons! Let him in.
25      Stay, help me off, first, with my gown. Away,
Madam, to your withdrawing chamber.

[*Exit Doll.*]

                                                            Now,
In a new tune, new gesture, but old language.
This fellow is sent, from one negotiates with me
About the stone, too, for the holy brethren
30      Of Amsterdam, the exiled saints:³ that hope
To raise their discipline by it. I must use him
In some strange fashion, now, to make him admire me.


ACT 2, SCENE 5

([*Enter*] *Ananias*.)

SUBTLE.  Where is my drudge?
FACE.                                    Sir.
SUBTLE.                                        Take away the recipient,°   *condensing vessel*
And rectify your menstrue, from the phlegma.⁴

---

1   *Anabaptist*  Puritan sect that arose in Germany in 1521.
2   *gold-end man*  Buyer of ends and bits of gold and silver.
3   *exiled saints*  Dutch puritans (Anabaptists) who moved to England after facing resistance to
    their faith in Amsterdam.
4   *rectify ... phlegma*  Purify the solvent from the watery distillate.

Then pour it o' the *Sol*, in the cucurbite,[1]
And let them macerate,° together.                              *steep*
FACE.                              Yes, sir.                          5
And save the ground?
SUBTLE.                    No. *Terra damnata*°            *residue*
Must not have entrance in the work. (*To Ananias.*) Who are you?
ANANIAS. A faithful brother,[2] if it please you.
SUBTLE.                                        What's that?
A Lullianist? A Ripley? *Filius Artis*?[3]
Can you sublime and dulcify? Calcine?[4]                      10
Know you the *sapor pontic*? *Sapor styptic*?[5]
Or what is homogene, or heterogene?[6]
ANANIAS. I understand no heathen language, truly.
SUBTLE. Heathen, you Knipper-Doling? Is *Ars sacra*,[7]
Or chrysopoeia, or spagyrica,[8]                              15
Or the pamphysic, or panarchic knowledge,[9]
A heathen language?[10]
ANANIAS.                    Heathen Greek, I take it.
SUBTLE. How? Heathen Greek?
ANANIAS.                              All's heathen but the Hebrew.[11]
SUBTLE. Sirrah, my varlet, stand you forth, and speak to him
Like a philosopher: answer, i' the language.[12]
                                                              20
Name the vexations, and the martyrisations[13]

---

1  *Sol* Sun, representing gold;  *cucurbite* Gourd-shaped vessel.
2  *faithful brother* Anabaptists referred to each other this way. Subtle pretends to misunderstand and takes Ananias for a fellow believer in alchemy.
3  *Lullianist* Follower of Ramond Llull (1232–1315), Spanish courtier and reputed alchemist;  *Ripley* George Ripley (d.c. 1490) 15th-century popularizer of Llull, author of *The Compound of Alchemy*;  *Filius Artis* Latin: son of the art, i.e., an alchemist.
4  *dulcify* To wash the salts out of a substance and neutralize acidity;  *Calcine* For alchemists, this meant to reduce a metal to its purest residue.
5  *sapor pontic ... Sapor styptic* Two of the nine tastes engendered by heat and cold.
6  *homogene ... heterogene* Of one kind (homogenous) or of various kinds (heterogenous).
7  *Knipper-Doling* A leader of the Anabaptist uprising in Munster, 1534–36;  *Ars sacra* Sacred art (of alchemy).
8  *chrysopoeia* Gold-making;  *spagyrica* Word invented by Paracelsus for his alchemical method.
9  *pamphysic, or panarchic knowledge* Knowledge of all nature.
10  *heathen language* In this context, language spoken by people holding non-Christian beliefs.
11  *Hebrew* Not heathen because Hebrew was thought to be the language spoken by Adam.
12  *i' the language* In the language of alchemy.
13  *vexations ... martyrisations* Alchemical processes applied to metals.

Of metals in the work.

FACE.                 Sir, putrefaction,
Solution, ablution, sublimation,
Cohobation, calcination, ceration, and
Fixation.[1]

SUBTLE.      This is heathen Greek to you, now?

25   And when comes vivification?[2]

FACE.                  After mortification.[3]

SUBTLE. What's cohobation?°                 *redistillation*

FACE.              'Tis the pouring on
Your *aqua regis*,[4] and then drawing him off,
To the trine circle of the seven spheres.[5]

SUBTLE. What's the proper passion[6] of metals?

FACE.                    Malleation.°    *hammering*

30 SUBTLE. What's your *ultimum supplicium auri*?[7]

FACE.                   Antimonium.[8]

SUBTLE. This 's heathen Greek, to you? And what's your mercury?

FACE. A very fugitive, he will be gone, sir.

SUBTLE. How know you him?

FACE.               By his viscosity,°      *stickiness*
His oleosity, and his suscitability.[9]

35 SUBTLE. How do you sublime him?

FACE.              With the calce[10] of egg-shells,
White marble, talc.

SUBTLE.       Your *magisterium* now,
What's that?

FACE.       Shifting, sir, your elements,

---

1   *putrefaction ... Fixation* Stages in the alchemical process whereby metal is transformed, dissolved, purified, vaporized, redistilled, converted to powder, made into wax, and finally stabilized.

2   *vivification* Restoring a metal to its natural state.

3   *mortification* Alteration of metal away from its natural state.

4   *aqua regis* Acidic solvent for gold.

5   *trine circle of the seven spheres* Solution requiring three trips through the seven planets. "Trine" is the division of a circle (orbit) into three parts, giving planets a favorable aspect.

6   *proper passion* Distinguishing quality of a substance.

7   *ultimum supplicium auri* Extreme punishment for gold.

8   *Antimonium* Antimony destroys the malleability of gold.

9   *oleosity* Oiliness; *suscitability* Excitability.

10   *calce* Powder residue of burned metal.

Dry into cold, cold into moist, moist in-
    To hot, hot into dry.
SUBTLE.                    This's heathen Greek to you, still?
    Your *lapis philosophicus*?[1]                                                    40
FACE.                              'Tis a stone, and not
    A stone; a spirit, a soul, and a body:
    Which if you do dissolve, it is dissolved,
    If you coagulate, it is coagulated,
    If you make it to fly, it flieth.
SUBTLE.                         Enough.


[*Exit Face.*]


This's heathen Greek, to you? What are you, sir?                                   45
ANANIAS.  Please you, a servant of the exiled brethren,
    That deal with widows' and with orphans' goods,
    And make a just account, unto the saints:
    A deacon.
SUBTLE.        O, you are sent from Master Wholesome,
    Your teacher?                                                                   50
ANANIAS.          From Tribulation Wholesome,
    Our very zealous pastor.
SUBTLE.                        Good. I have
    Some orphans' goods to come here.
ANANIAS.                               Of what kind, sir?
SUBTLE.  Pewter, and brass, andirons, and kitchen ware,
    Metals, that we must use our med'cine on:
    Wherein the brethren may have a penn'orth[2]                                    55
    For ready money.
ANANIAS.              Were the orphans' parents
    Sincere professors?°                                            *good puritans*
SUBTLE.            Why do you ask?
ANANIAS.                            Because
    We then are to deal justly, and give (in truth)

---

1  *lapis philosophicus*  Philosopher's stone.
2  *penn'orth*  As much as can be purchased for a penny.

Their utmost value.

SUBTLE.                          'Slid, you'd cozen else,

60    And if their parents were not of the faithful?
      I will not trust you, now I think on't,
      Till I have talked with your pastor. Ha' you brought money
      To buy more coals?

ANANIAS.                    No, surely.

SUBTLE.                               No? How so?

ANANIAS.  The brethren bid me say unto you, sir,

65    Surely they will not venture any more,
      Till they may see projection.

SUBTLE.                         How!

ANANIAS.                              You've had,

      For the instruments, as bricks, and loam, and glasses,
      Already thirty pound; and for materials,
      They say, some ninety more: and, they have heard, since,

70    That one at Heidelberg,¹ made it of an egg,
      And a small paper of pin-dust.°                      *metal filings*

SUBTLE.                         What's your name?

ANANIAS.  My name is Ananias.

SUBTLE.                         Out, the varlet

      That cozen'd the Apostles!² Hence, away,
      Flee, Mischief; had your holy consistory°           *puritan assembly*

75    No name to send me, of another sound,
      Than wicked Ananias? Send your Elders°              *church officers*
      Hither, to make atonement for you, quickly,
      And gi' me satisfaction; or out goes
      The fire: and down th' alembics, and the furnace,

80    *Piger Henricus,*³ or what not. Thou wretch,
      Both *sericon* and *bufo,*⁴ shall be lost,
      Tell 'em. All hope of rooting out the bishops,

---

1   *Heidelberg*  German center of alchemical experimentation.
2   *varlet ... Apostles*  Ananias tried to cheat the apostles by holding back a portion of the
    proceeds from the sale of his property and immediately fell down dead (Acts 5.1–6). It
    is also the name of the high priest at the time of Paul's trials in Jerusalem and Caesarea
    (Acts 23.2).
3   *Piger Henricus*  The "lazy Henry," a furnace with multiple compartments.
4   *sericon and bufo*  Red tincture and black tincture.

Or th'antichristian hierarchy, [1] shall perish,
If they stay threescore minutes. The aqueity,
Terreity, and sulphureity[2]                                                    85
Shall run together again, and all be annull'd,
Thou wicked Ananias.

[*Exit Ananias.*]

                                        This will fetch 'em,
And make 'em haste towards their gulling more.
A man must deal like a rough nurse, and fright
Those that are froward to an appetite.[3]                                        90


                          ACT 2, Scene 6

([*Enter*] *Face* [*and*] *Drugger.*)

FACE.  [*To Drugger.*] He's busy with his spirits,[4] but we'll upon him.
SUBTLE.  How now! What mates? What Bayards[5] ha' we here?
FACE.  [*To Drugger.*] I told you, he would be furious.  Sir, here's Nab,
   Has brought you another piece of gold to look on:
   [*Aside to Drugger.*] We must appease him. Give it me.—And prays   5
      you,
   You would devise—[*Aside to Drugger.*] What is it, Nab?
DRUGGER.                                              A sign, sir.
FACE.  Ay, a good lucky one, a thriving sign, Doctor.
SUBTLE.  I was devising now.
FACE.  [*Aside to Subtle.*]        'Slight, do not say so,
   He will repent he ga' you any more.—

---

1   *rooting out … antichristian hierarchy*   Radical reformers such as the Anabaptists advocated
    against "popish" hierarchy in the Church of England, and they argued for the removal of
    bishops in particular.
2   *aqueity*   Water quality; *Terreity*   Earth quality; *sulphureity*   Sulphur quality.
3   *fright Those … froward to an appetite*   Scare those that are fractious or contrary (froward) to
    a desire for more.
4   *spirits*   Distilled essences or supernatural beings.
5   *mates*   Low persons; *Bayards*   Common name for horses, after Charlemagne's legendary
    steed. The term "Bayard" came to stand for blindness or ignorance, and Subtle is using it
    thus, as an insult.

10   What say you to his constellation,° Doctor?          *zodiac sign*
     The Balance?°                                          *Libra*
SUBTLE.          No, that way is stale, and common.
     A townsman, born in Taurus,[1] gives the bull,
     Or the bull's head: in Aries,[2] the ram.
     A poor device. No, I will have his name
15   Formed in some mystic character; whose radii,[3]
     Striking the senses of the passers by,
     Shall, by a virtual influence, breed affections,
     That may result upon the party owns it:
     As thus—
FACE.          Nab!
SUBTLE.          He first shall have a bell, that's "A-bel;"[4]
20   And, by it, standing one, whose name is Dee,[5]
     In a rug gown;[6] there's D and Rug, that's "Drug;"
     And, right anenst° him, a dog snarling, "Er";          *opposite*
     There's "Drugger," "Abel Drugger." That's his sign.
     And here's now mystery and hieroglyphic![7]
25 FACE. Abel, thou art made.
   DRUGGER.                    Sir, I do thank his worship.
   FACE. Six o' thy legs° more, will not do it, Nab.          *bows*
     He has brought you a pipe of tobacco, Doctor.
   DRUGGER.                              Yes, sir;
     I have another thing I would impart—
   FACE. Out with it, Nab.
   DRUGGER.          Sir, there is lodged, hard by me,
30   A rich young widow—
   FACE.                    Good! a *bona roba*?[8]

---

1   *Taurus*   Sign symbolized by the bull.
2   *Aries*   Sign symbolized by the ram.
3   *radii*   Emanations.
4   *a bell, that's A-bel*   Subtle is creating a rebus of Abel Drugger's name (a cryptic, symbolic version of the name).
5   *Dee*   Dr. John Dee (1527–1608), mathematician and astronomer whose interests extended to astrology and alchemy.
6   *rug gown*   A gown made of rug.
7   *hieroglyphic*   Subtle is saying his sign for Drugger is of the nature of hieroglyphs, concealing hidden meanings within pictures or symbols.
8   *bona roba*   Well-dressed; it can also mean prostitute.

DRUGGER. But nineteen, at the most.

FACE. Very good, Abel.

DRUGGER. Marry, she's not in fashion, yet; she wears
   A hood: but 't stands acop.[1]

FACE. No matter, Abel.

DRUGGER. And—I do now and then give her a fucus—[2]

FACE. What! Dost thou deal,[3] Nab?                                35

SUBTLE. I did tell you, Captain.

DRUGGER. And physic too, sometime, sir; for which she trusts me
   With all her mind. She's come up here, of purpose
   To learn the fashion.

FACE. Good—[*Aside.*] His match[4] too!—On, Nab.

DRUGGER. And she does strangely° long to know her fortune.    *greatly*

FACE. God's lid, Nab, send her to the Doctor, hither.              40

DRUGGER. Yes, I have spoke to her of his worship, already;
   But she's afraid it will be blown abroad,°          *rumored about*
   And hurt her marriage.[5]

FACE. Hurt it? 'Tis the way
   To heal it, if 'twere hurt; to make it more
   Followed, and sought: Nab, thou shalt tell her this.         45
   She'll be more known, more talked of, and your widows
   Are ne'er of any price till they be famous;
   Their honour is their multitude of suitors:
   Send her, it may be thy good fortune. What?
   Thou dost not know.                                    50

DRUGGER. No, sir, she'll never marry
   Under a knight. Her brother has made a vow.

FACE. What, and dost thou despair, my little Nab,
   Knowing what the Doctor has set down for thee,
   And seeing so many, o' the city, dubbed?°          *knighted*
   One glass o' thy water, with a Madam I know,         55
   Will have it done, Nab. What's her brother? A knight?

---

1   *acop*  On top of the head (hoods were out of fashion).

2   *fucus*  Cosmetic for the skin, with an implied sexual innuendo.

3   *deal*  Do business, though "deal" can also mean "copulate," carrying on the sexual subtext
   of "fucus."

4   *his match*  One who is as big a fool as he is.

5   *marriage*  Marriage prospects.

DRUGGER. No, sir, a gentleman, newly warm in his land,[1] sir,
    Scarce cold in his one and twenty; that does govern
    His sister, here: and is a man himself
60    Of some three thousand a year, and is come up
    To learn to quarrel, and to live by his wits,
    And will go down again and die i' the country.
FACE. How! To quarrel?
DRUGGER.               Yes, sir, to carry quarrels,
    As gallants do, and manage 'em, by line.[2]
65 FACE. 'Slid, Nab! The Doctor is the only man
    In Christendom for him. He has made a table,°      *diagram*
    With mathematical demonstrations,
    Touching the art of quarrels. He will give him
    An instrument to quarrel by. Go, bring 'em both,
70    Him and his sister. And, for thee, with her
    The Doctor happ'ly° may persuade. Go to.     *by chance*
    'Shalt give his worship a new damask suit[3]
    Upon the premises.°                     *prospects*
SUBTLE.          Oh, good Captain.
FACE.                         He shall;
    He is the honestest fellow, Doctor. Stay not,
75 No offers, bring the damask, and the parties.
DRUGGER. I'll try my power, sir.
FACE.               And thy will too, Nab.
SUBTLE. 'Tis good tobacco this! What is 't an ounce?
FACE. He'll send you a pound, Doctor.
SUBTLE.              Oh, no.
FACE.                     He will do 't.
    It is the goodest soul. Abel, about it.
80 [*Aside to Drugger.*] Thou shalt know more anon. Away, be gone.

[*Exit Drugger.*]

    A miserable rogue, and lives with cheese,
    And has the worms. That was the cause indeed,

---

1   *newly warm in his land*  Having just inherited his land.
2   *by line*  According to the rules of gallantry and the courtly code of dueling.
3   *damask suit*  Suit of richly embroidered linen.

Why he came now. He dealt with me, in private,
To get a med'cine for 'em.

SUBTLE.                            And shall, sir. This works.

FACE.  A wife, a wife for one on us, my dear Subtle:            85
We'll e'en draw lots, and he that fails shall have
The more in goods the other has in tail.[1]

SUBTLE.  Rather the less: for she may be so light°            *loose*
She may want grains.°                                          *weight*

FACE.                            Aye, or be such a burden,
A man would scarce endure her, for the whole.               90

SUBTLE.  Faith, best let's see her first, and then determine.

FACE.  Content. But Doll must ha' no breath on 't.

SUBTLE.                                        Mum.
Away, you, to your Surly yonder. Catch him.

FACE.  Pray God, I ha' not stayed too long.

SUBTLE.                                        I fear it.

[*Exeunt.*]

## ACT 3, SCENE I

([*Enter*] *Tribulation* [*and*] *Ananias*.)

TRIBULATION.  These chastisements are common to the Saints,
And such rebukes we of the separation[2]
Must bear, with willing shoulders, as the trials
Sent forth, to tempt our frailties.

ANANIAS.                            In pure zeal,
I do not like the man: he is a heathen.                       5
And speaks the language of Canaan,[3] truly.

---

1  *in tail*  Tying up the land succession (entail), with a sexual pun.
2  *the separation*  Both physical (exiled from the continent) and spiritual (the elect chosen by God).
3  *Canaan*  Ancient name for land promised by God to Abraham and inhabited by the Israelites; the name also refers to the ancient group of languages, including Hebrew, spoken in ancient Palestine.

TRIBULATION. I think him a profane person indeed.
ANANIAS.                                  He bears
  The visible mark of the Beast,[1] in his forehead.
  And for his stone, it is a work of darkness,
10   And, with philosophy, blinds the eyes of man.
TRIBULATION. Good brother, we must bend unto all means,
  That may give furtherance to the holy cause.
ANANIAS. Which his cannot: the sanctified cause
  Should have a sanctified course.
TRIBULATION.                Not always necessary.
15   The children of perdition are, oft-times,
  Made instruments even of the greatest works.
  Beside, we should give° somewhat to man's nature,       *be flexible*
  The place he lives in, still about the fire,
  And fume of metals, that intoxicate
20   The brain of man, and make him prone to passion.
  Where have you greater atheists than your cooks?
  Or more profane or choleric than your glass-men?°     *glass blowers*
  More antichristian, than your bell-founders?°       *bell makers*
  What makes the devil so devilish, I would ask you,
25   Satan, our common enemy, but his being
  Perpetually about the fire, and boiling
  Brimstone and ars'nic? We must give, I say,
  Unto the motives, and the stirrers up
  Of humours in the blood. It may be so;
30   When as the work is done, the stone is made,
  This heat of his may turn into a zeal,
  And stand up for the beauteous discipline,
  Against the menstruous cloth, and rag of Rome.[2]
  We must await his calling, and the coming
35   Of the good spirit. You did fault, t' upbraid him
  With the brethren's blessing of Heidelberg, weighing
  What need we have to hasten on the work,

---

1   *mark of the Beast*   The mark of the damned in the visions of judgment at the end of time
  in Revelation 16.2, 19.20.
2   *menstruous cloth, and rag of Rome*   Crude reference to the Whore of Babylon, "the mother
  of all harlots," an image of the fallen city in Revelation (17.1,5; 18.3).

For the restoring of the silenced saints,[1]
Which ne'er will be, but by the philosopher's stone.
And so a learnèd elder, one of Scotland,[2]                    40
Assured me; *aurum potabile°* being          *drinkable gold (i.e., a bribe)*
The only med'cine, for the civil magistrate,
T' incline him to a feeling of the cause;
And must be daily used in the disease.

ANANIAS.  I have not edified[3] more, truly, by man;          45
Not since the beautiful light first shone on me:
And I am sad my zeal hath so offended.

TRIBULATION.  Let us call on him, then.

ANANIAS.                    The motion's° good,          *impulse*
And of the spirit; I will knock first: peace be within.


ACT 3, SCENE 2

(*[Enter] Subtle.*)

SUBTLE.  O, are you come? 'Twas time. Your threescore° minutes          *sixty*
Were at last thread, you see; and down had gone
*Furnus acediae, turris circulatorius:*[4]
Limbec, bolt's-head, retort, and pelican[5]
Had all been cinders. Wicked Ananias!                    5
Art thou returned? Nay then, it goes down, yet.

TRIBULATION.  Sir, be appeased; he is come to humble
Himself in spirit, and to ask your patience,
If too much zeal hath carried him aside,
From the due path.                    10

SUBTLE.                    Why, this doth qualify![6]

TRIBULATION.  The brethren had no purpose, verily,
To give you the least grievance: but are ready
To lend their willing hands, to any project

---

1  *silenced saints*  Puritan clergy who were not allowed to preach.
2  *Scotland*  Puritans had more success with church reform in Scotland than in England.
3  *edified*  Gained instruction.
4  *Furnus acediae*  Furnace of sloth;  *turris circulatorius*  Circulating tower.
5  *Limbec ... pelican*  These are all apparatuses for distillation.
6  *qualify*  Lessen my anger; dilute my liquid.

The spirit and you direct.
SUBTLE.                        This qualifies more!
15 TRIBULATION. And, for the orphans' goods, let them be valued,
    Or what is needful else to the holy work,
    It shall be numbered: here, by me, the saints
    Throw down their purse before you.
SUBTLE.                        This qualifies most!
    Why, thus it should be, now you understand.
20 Have I discoursed so unto you, of our stone?
    And of the good that it shall bring your cause?
    Showed you (beside the main of hiring forces
    Abroad, drawing the Hollanders, your friends,
    From th' Indies, to serve you, with all their fleet[1])
25 That even the med'cinal use shall make you a faction,
    And party in the realm? As, put the case,
    That some great man in state, he have the gout,
    Why you but send three drops of your elixir,
    You help him straight: there you have made a friend.
30 Another has the palsy, or the dropsy,[2]
    He takes of your incombustible[3] stuff,
    He's young again: there you have made a friend,
    A lady that is past the feat of body,°            *sexual intercourse*
    Though not of mind, and hath her face decayed
35 Beyond all cure of paintings,° you restore,        *makeup*
    With the oil of talc;[4] there you have made a friend:
    And all her friends. A lord, that is a leper,
    A knight, that has the bone-ache,° or a squire     *syphilis*
    That hath both these, you make 'em smooth, and sound,
40 With a bare fricace° of your med'cine: still,        *application*
    You increase your friends.
TRIBULATION.                        Aye, 'tis very pregnant.

---

1  *Hollanders ... fleet* The Anabaptists were assisted by the Dutch navy when they fled Germany.
2  *palsy* Paralysis, tremor; *dropsy* Condition in which fluid accumulates in the body.
3  *incombustible* Impervious to fire.
4  *oil of talc* Alchemical cosmetic preparation.

SUBTLE. And then, the turning of this lawyer's pewter
   To plate, at Christmas—
ANANIAS.                 "Christ-tide,"[1] I pray you.
SUBTLE. Yet, Ananias?
ANANIAS.         I have done.
SUBTLE.                   Or changing
   His parcel gilt,° to massy° gold. You cannot     *gold plated / solid*  45
   But raise you friends. With all, to be of power
   To pay an army in the field; to buy
   The King of France, out of his realms; or Spain
   Out of his Indies: what can you not do
   Against lords spiritual, or temporal,                 50
   That shall oppose you?
TRIBULATION.         Verily, 'tis true.
   We may be temporal lords ourselves, I take it.
SUBTLE. You may be anything, and leave off to make
   Long-winded exercises:° or suck up          *puritan sermons*
   Your ha, and hum,[2] in a tune. I not deny,          55
   But such as are not graced, in a state,
   May, for their ends, be adverse in religion,
   And get a tune, to call the flock together:
   For, to say sooth, a tune does much, with women,
   And other phlegmatic people; it is your bell.        60
ANANIAS. Bells are profane:[3] a tune may be religious.
SUBTLE. No warning with you?[4] Then, farewell my patience.
   'Slight, it shall down: I will not be thus tortured.
TRIBULATION. I pray you, sir.
SUBTLE.             All shall perish. I have spoke it.
TRIBULATION. Let me find grace, sir, in your eyes; the man    65
   He stands corrected: neither did his zeal
   But as yourself, allow a tune, somewhere.
   Which now, being toward the stone,[5] we shall not need.

---

- 1  *Christ-tide*  Alternative way of saying "Christmas," which avoids using what the Anabaptists viewed as the Popish "mas" (mass).
- 2  *ha, and hum*  Sounds often made by Anabaptists during prayer.
- 3  *Bells are profane*  Puritans link the sounding of bells to Popish liturgical habits.
- 4  *No ... you?*  Is there no point in giving you a warning?
- 5  *toward the stone*  On the way to getting the stone.

SUBTLE. No, nor your holy vizard,° to win widows      *mask*
70   To give you legacies; or make zealous wives
To rob their husbands, for the common cause:
Nor take the start of bonds,¹ broke but one day,
And say, they were forfeited, by providence.
Nor shall you need o'er-night to eat huge meals,
75   To celebrate your next day's fast the better:
The whilst the brethren, and the sisters, humbled,
Abate the stiffness of the flesh. Nor cast
Before your hungry hearers, scrupulous bones,²
As whether a Christian may hawk, or hunt,
80   Or whether matrons, of the holy assembly
May lay their hair out, or wear doublets,³
Or have that idol starch,⁴ about their linen.
ANANIAS. It is, indeed, an idol.
TRIBULATION. [*To Subtle.*]     Mind him not, sir.
[*To Ananias.*] I do command thee, spirit of zeal, but trouble,
85   To peace within him. [*To Subtle.*] Pray you, sir, go on.
SUBTLE. Nor shall you need to libel 'gainst the prelates,
And shorten so your ears,⁵ against the hearing
Of the next wire-drawn° grace. Nor, of necessity     *drawn out*
Rail against plays, to please the alderman,
90   Whose daily custard⁶ you devour. Nor lie
With zealous rage, till you are hoarse. Not one
Of these so singular arts. Nor call yourselves
By names of Tribulation, Persecution,
Restraint, Long-patience, and such-like, affected
95   By the whole family or wood° of you,     *collection*
Only for glory, and to catch the ear
Of the disciple.
TRIBULATION.     Truly, sir, they are

---

1  *take ... bonds*  Take advantage by claiming the bonds to be forfeit.
2  *scrupulous bones*  Petty arguments about trivial matters.
3  *wear doublets*  C.f. Deuteronomy 22.5: "a woman shall not wear anything that pertains to a man." A doublet is a close-fitting jacket worn by men in the Renaissance.
4  *idol starch*  Anabaptists opposed the use of starch on clothing as vain and idolatrous.
5  *shorten so your ears*  Have your ears clipped or cut off as punishment.
6  *custard*  Open pie served at civic receptions.

Ways that the godly brethren have invented,
For propagation of the glorious cause,
As very notable means, and whereby, also          100
Themselves grow soon, and profitably famous.
SUBTLE. O, but the stone, all's idle to it! Nothing!
    The art of angels, Nature's miracle,
    The divine secret that doth fly in clouds
    From east to west: and whose tradition          105
    Is not from men, but spirits.
ANANIAS.                    I hate traditions:
    I do not trust them—
TRIBULATION.          Peace.
ANANIAS.                They are Popish, all.
    I will not peace. I will not—
TRIBULATION.                Ananias!
ANANIAS. Please the profane, to grieve the godly: I may not.
SUBTLE. Well, Ananias, thou shalt overcome.          110
TRIBULATION. It is an ignorant zeal that haunts him, sir;
    But truly, else, a very faithful brother,
    A botcher:° and a man, by revelation,[1]          *clothes mender*
    That hath a competent knowledge of the truth.
SUBTLE. Has he a competent sum, there i' the bag,          115
    To buy the goods, within? I am made guardian,
    And must, for charity, and conscience sake,
    Now, see the most be made, for my poor orphans:
    Though I desire the brethren, too, good gainers.
    There they are, within. When you have viewed and bought 'em,          120
    And ta'en the inventory of what they are,
    They are ready for projection;[2] there's no more
    To do: cast on the med'cine, so much silver
    As there is tin there, so much gold as brass,
    I'll gi' it you in, by weight.[3]          125
TRIBULATION.                But how long time,

---

1   *by revelation*   By direct inspiration from the Bible.
2   *projection*   Casting of powdered philosopher's stone onto metal to transform it to gold.
3   *I'll gi' it you in, by weight*   Exchange it weight for weight.

   Sir, must the Saints expect,° yet?                    *wait*

SUBTLE.                   Let me see,

   How's the moon now? Eight, nine, ten days hence

   He will be silver potate;° then three days,       *liquid silver*

   Before he citronise:° some fifteen days,        *turn yellow*

130   The *magisterium* will be perfected.

ANANIAS.  About the second day, of the third week,

   In the ninth month?

SUBTLE.            Yes, my good Ananias.

TRIBULATION.  What will the orphans' goods arise to, think you?

SUBTLE.  Some hundred marks;[1] as much as filled three cars,°   *carts*

135  Unladed° now: you'll make six millions of 'em.     *unloaded*

   But I must ha' more coals laid in.

TRIBULATION.             How!

SUBTLE.                  Another load,

   And then we ha' finish'd. We must now increase

   Our fire to *ignis ardens*, we are past

   *Fimus equinus, balnei, cineris*,[2]

140  And all those lenter° heats. If the holy purse       *slower*

   Should, with this draught, fall low, and that the saints

   Do need a present sum, I have a trick

   To melt the pewter, you shall buy now, instantly,

   And with a tincture, make you as good Dutch dollars°   *silver coins*

145  As any are in Holland.

TRIBULATION.          Can you so?

SUBTLE.  Aye, and shall bide the third examination.[3]

ANANIAS.  It will be joyful tidings to the brethren.

SUBTLE.  But you must carry it secret.

TRIBULATION.               Aye, but stay,

   This act of coining, is it lawful?

ANANIAS.              Lawful?

150  We know° no magistrate, or, if we did,          *recognize*

---

1   *marks*  Measures of weight for gold and silver; each mark equals about 8 ounces.

2   *ignis ardens ... Fimus equinus, balnei, cineris*  Sequence of heats in alchemy that vary in temperature and intensity: hottest, slowest (fueled by horse dung), heated baths, and warm sand or ashes, respectively.

3   *bide ... examination*  Pass three inspections (counterfeited money so convincing that three inspections won't reveal the fraud).

This 's foreign coin.

SUBTLE.                    It is no coining, sir.
   It is but casting.¹
TRIBULATION.       Ha? You distinguish well.
   Casting of money may be lawful.
ANANIAS.                            'Tis, sir.
TRIBULATION.  Truly, I take it so.
SUBTLE.                            There is no scruple,                    155
   Sir, to be made of it; believe Ananias:
   This case of conscience he is studied in.
TRIBULATION.  I'll make a question of it, to the brethren.
ANANIAS.  The brethren shall approve it lawful, doubt not.
   Where shall 't be done?
SUBTLE.                    For that we'll talk anon.

   (*Knock without.*)

There's some to speak with me. Go in, I pray you,                    160
And view the parcels. That's the inventory.
I'll come to you straight.

   [*Exeunt Tribulation and Ananias.*]

   [*Calling.*]                    Who is it? Face! Appear.


ACT 3, Scene 3


(*Enter Face.*)

SUBTLE.  How now! Good prize?
FACE.                    Good pox! Yond' costive° cheater²    *constipated*

---

1   *casting*   Casting coins in a mould.
2   *cheater*   I.e., Surly.

Never came on.°                        *showed up*
SUBTLE.         How then?
FACE.                I ha' walked the round,°    *kept a lookout*
   Till now, and no such thing.[1]
SUBTLE.             And ha' you quit him?
FACE.   Quit him? An hell would quit him too, he were happy.
5    'Slight would you have me stalk like a mill-jade,[2]
   All day, for one, that will not yield us grains?°           *profit*
   I know him of old.
SUBTLE.           O, but to ha' gulled him,
   Had been a mastery.
FACE.             Let him go, black boy,[3]
   And turn thee,[4] that some fresh news may possess thee.
10   A noble Count, a Don of Spain (my dear
   Delicious compeer, and my party-bawd,°)       *fellow pimp*
   Who is come hither, private, for his conscience,
   And brought munition with him, six great slops,°     *trousers*
   Bigger than three Dutch hoys,° beside round trunks,[5]   *ships*
15   Furnished with pistolets, and pieces of eight,[6]
   Will straight be here, my rogue, to have thy bath,[7]
   (That is the colour)° and to make his battery       *pretext*
   Upon our Doll, our castle, our Cinque Port,[8]
   Our Dover pier, our what thou wilt. Where is she?
20   She must prepare perfumes, delicate linen,
   The bath in chief,° a banquet, and her wit,        *especially*
   For she must milk his epididimis.°      *make him ejaculate*

---

1   *no such thing*   I.e., he never appeared.
2   *mill-jade*   Tethered horse that would drive the grindstone in a mill, by walking round and round in a circle.
3   *black boy*   Subtle is wearing black robes and his face is sooty from the furnace (could also be referring to Surly, in which case this could mean "blackguard" or scoundrel).
4   *turn thee*   Shift your attention.
5   *round trunks*   Blowsy pants worn in the 16th and 17th centuries, covering the hips and thighs and sometimes stuffed with wool.
6   *pistolets*   Spanish gold coins; *pieces of eight*   Spanish silver coins.
7   *bath*   It was customary in some brothels for customers to have a bath before sex with a prostitute.
8   *Cinque Port*   Coastal towns, literally "five ports," in Kent and Sussex. The towns lie where the channel between England and France is narrowest, so the ports were important for trade.

Where is the doxy?°                                                   *whore*
SUBTLE.               I'll send her to thee:
  And but despatch my brace of little John Leydens,[1]
  And come again myself.                                               25
FACE.                  Are they within then?
SUBTLE.  Numbering the sum.
FACE.                  How much?
SUBTLE.                          A hundred marks, boy.

[*Exit.*]

FACE.  Why, this 's a lucky day! Ten pounds of Mammon!
  Three o' my clerk! A portague[2] o' my grocer!
  This o' the brethren! Beside reversions,[3]
  And states° to come i' the widow, and my Count!        *estates*  30
  My share, today, will not be bought for forty—

([*Enter*] *Doll.*)

DOLL.                                                What?
FACE.  Pounds, dainty Dorothy, art thou so near?
DOLL.  Yes, say, lord general, how fares our camp?
FACE.  As, with the few, that had entrenched themselves
  Safe, by their discipline, against a world, Doll:                   35
  And laughed within those trenches, and grew fat
  With thinking on the booties, Doll, brought in
  Daily, by their small parties. This dear hour,
  A doughty Don is taken, with my Doll;
  And thou mayst make his ransom, what thou wilt,                     40
  My dousabel:[4] he shall be brought here, fettered
  With thy fair looks, before he sees thee; and thrown
  In a down-bed, as dark as any dungeon;
  Where thou shalt keep him waking, with thy drum;
  Thy drum, my Doll; thy drum; till he be tame                       45
  As the poor black-birds were i' the great frost,°       *of 1607–08*

---

1  *John Leydens*  Puritans, after a leader of a 16th-century Anabaptist uprising.
2  *portague*  Portuguese gold coin.
3  *reversions*  Benefits yet to come after the death of the present owner.
4  *dousabel*  I.e., *Douce et belle* (French), sweet and pretty.

Or bees are with a basin:[1] and so hive him
I' the swan-skin coverlid, and cambric sheets,
Till he work honey and wax, my little God's-gift.[2]
50 DOLL. What is he, General?
FACE.                              An *adalantado*,°               *Spanish dignitary*
A grandee, girl. Was not my Dapper here, yet?
DOLL. No.
FACE.              Nor my Drugger?
DOLL.                              Neither.
FACE.                                        A pox on 'em,
They are so long a furnishing!° Such stinkards              *getting ready*
Would° not be seen, upon these festival days.              *should*

[*Enter Subtle.*]

55 How now! Ha' you done?
SUBTLE.                              Done. They are gone. The sum
Is here in bank,° my Face. I would we knew              *our possession*
Another chapman, now, would buy 'em outright.
FACE. 'Slid, Nab shall do't, against he ha' the widow,
To furnish household.
SUBTLE.              Excellent, well thought on,
60 Pray God, he come.
FACE.                              I pray, he keep away
Till our new business be o'erpast.
SUBTLE.                                        But Face,
How cam'st thou by this secret Don?
FACE.                                        A spirit
Brought me th' intelligence, in a paper, here,
As I was conjuring, yonder, in my circle
65 For Surly: I ha' my flies° abroad. Your bath              *spies*
Is famous, Subtle, by my means. Sweet Doll,
You must go tune your virginal,[3] no losing
O' the least time. And, do you hear? Good action.

---

1  *bees are with a basin*  It was thought that if one banged on a basin, bees would return to the hive.
2  *God's-gift*  Doll's full name, Dorothea, means "God's gift" in Greek.
3  *tune your virginal*  Sexual innuendo. A virginal is a harpsichord.

Firk,[1] like a flounder; kiss, like a scallop, close:
And tickle him with thy mother-tongue. His great                    70
Verdugoship has not a jot of language:[2]
So much the easier to be cozened, my Dolly.
He will come here in a hired coach, obscure,°              *privately*
And our own coachman, whom I have sent as guide,
No creature else.                                                   75

(*One knocks.*)

                    Who's that?
SUBTLE.                   It i' not he?
FACE.  O no, not yet this hour.
SUBTLE.                  Who is 't?
DOLL.  [*Looking out.*]          Dapper,
  Your clerk.
FACE.       God's will, then, Queen of Fairy,
  On with your tire.°                                       *attire*

[*Exit Doll.*]

And, Doctor, with your robes.
Let's dispatch him, for God's sake.
SUBTLE.                'Twill be long.
FACE.  I warrant you, take but the cues I give you,           80
  It shall be brief enough. [*Looking out.*] 'Slight, here are more!
  Abel, and I think, the angry boy,[3] the heir,
  That fain would quarrel.
SUBTLE.           And the widow?
FACE.                No,
  Not that I see. Away. [*Exit Subtle.*]
          Oh, sir, you are welcome.

---

1  *Firk*  Play, rouse, excite (with a sexual pun).
2  *Verdugoship*  His Hangmanship (*Verdugo* is a Spanish word meaning "hangman");
  *language*  English.
3  *angry boy*  Kastril, who wants to learn how to quarrel.

# ACT 3, SCENE 4

([*Enter*] *Dapper.*)

FACE. The Doctor is within, a-moving° for you            *working*
    I have had the most ado to win him to it;
    He swears, you'll be the darling o' the dice:
    He never heard her Highness dote, till now he says.
5    Your aunt has giv'n you the most gracious words
    That can be thought on.
DAPPER.                 Shall I see her Grace?
FACE.  See her, and kiss her, too.

([*Enter*] *Drugger* [*and*] *Kastril.*)
                         What? Honest Nab!
    Hast brought the damask?
DRUGGER.            No, sir, here's tobacco.
FACE.  'Tis well done, Nab: thou'lt bring the damask too?
10  DRUGGER.  Yes, here's the gentleman, Captain, master Kastril,
    I have brought to see the Doctor.
FACE.                 Where's the widow?
DRUGGER.  Sir, as he likes, his sister, he says, shall come.
FACE.  O, is it so? Good time. Is your name Kastril, sir?
KASTRIL.  Aye, and the best o' the Kastrils, I'd be sorry else,
15    By fifteen hundred, a year. Where is this Doctor?
    My mad tobacco boy here tells me of one,
    That can do things. Has he any skill?
FACE.                 Wherein, sir?
KASTRIL.  To carry a business, manage a quarrel fairly,
    Upon fit terms.
FACE.           It seems sir, you're but young
20    About the town, that can make that a question!
KASTRIL.  Sir, not so young, but I have heard some speech
    Of the angry boys,° and seen 'em take tobacco;        *hooligans*
    And in his shop: and I can take it too.
    And I would fain be one of 'em, and go down

And practise i' the country.[1]                                              25
FACE.                          Sir, for the duello,°                    *duel*
The Doctor, I assure you, shall inform you
To the least shadow of a hair: and show you
An instrument he has, of his own making,
Wherewith, no sooner shall you make report
Of any quarrel, but he will take the height on 't,                          30
Most instantly: and tell in what degree
Of safety it lies in, or mortality.
And how it may be borne, whether in a right line,
Or a half circle; or may, else, be cast
Into an angle blunt, if not acute:                                          35
All this he will demonstrate. And then, rules,
To give, and take the lie by.
KASTRIL.                        How? To take it?
FACE. Yes, in oblique he'll show you; or in circle:
But never in diameter.[2] The whole town
Study his theorems, and dispute them, ordinarily,                           40
At the eating academies.°                          *taverns, ordinaries*
KASTRIL.                    But—does he teach
Living by the wits, too?
FACE.                          Anything, whatever.
You cannot think that subtlety, but he reads it.
He made me a captain. I was a stark pimp,
Just o' your standing, 'fore I met with him:                                45
It i' not two months since. I'll tell you his method.
First, he will enter° you, at some ordinary.             *introduce*
KASTRIL. No, I'll not come there. You shall pardon me.
FACE.                                      For why, sir?
KASTRIL. There's gaming there, and tricks.
FACE.                              Why, would you be

---

1  *I would ... country*  The science of dueling, as well as the instructors in it, were frequent
   topics of satire in Jonson's day.
2  *oblique ... diameter*  Degrees of lie—falsehood—that spark different kinds of duel; the
   "oblique" lie is the "lie circumstantial"; the lie "in diameter" is the "lie direct." Face is saying
   that Subtle can give Kastril all the information he needs to know about how to lie and how
   to take lies, within the complex rules of dueling.

50    A gallant, and not game?

KASTRIL.                Aye, 'twill spend a man.[1]

FACE.  Spend you? It will repair you when you are spent.
    How do they live by their wits, there, that have vented°       *blown*
    Six times your fortunes?

KASTRIL.            What, three thousand a year!

FACE.  Aye, forty thousand.

KASTRIL.           Are there such?

FACE.                         Aye, sir,

55    And gallants, yet. Here's a young gentleman
    Is born to nothing, forty marks a year,
    Which I count nothing. He's to be initiated,
    And have a fly o' the Doctor. He will win you,
    By unresistible luck, within this fortnight,

60    Enough to buy a barony. They will set him
    Upmost, at the groom-porter's,[2] all the Christmas!
    And for the whole year through, at every place
    Where there is play, present him with the chair;
    The best attendance, the best drink, sometimes

65    Two glasses of Canary,° and pay nothing;          *sweet wine*
    The purest linen, and the sharpest knife,
    The partridge next his trencher:° and somewhere    *wooden plate*
    The dainty bed, in private, with the dainty.
    You shall ha' your ordinaries bid for him,

70    As play-houses for a poet; and the master
    Pray him, aloud, to name what dish he affects,°      *desires*
    Which must be buttered shrimps: and those that drink
    To no mouth else, will drink to his, as being
    The goodly, president mouth of all the board.

75  KASTRIL.  Do you not gull one?

FACE.               'Ods° my life! Do you think it?    *God's*
    You shall have a cast° commander (can but get    *dismissed*
    In credit with a glover, or a spurrier,°         *spur maker*
    For some two pair, of either's ware, aforehand)°    *on credit*
    Will, by most swift posts,[3] dealing with him,

---

1  *spend a man*  Waste a man's money or wealth.
2  *groom-porter*  Royal officer in charge of gaming.
3  *by most swift posts*  Very rapidly.

Arrive at competent means, to keep himself, 80
His punk, and naked boy,° in excellent fashion,      *male prostitute*
And be admir'd for 't.
KASTRIL.            Will the Doctor teach this?
FACE.  He will do more, sir, when your land is gone,
(As men of spirit hate to keep earth long),
In a vacation,° when small money is stirring,      *between law terms* 85
And ordinaries suspended till the term,
He'll show a perspective,¹ where on one side
You shall behold the faces, and the persons
Of all sufficient young heirs, in town,
Whose bonds are current for commodity;      90
On th' other side, the merchants' forms, and others,
That, without help of any second broker,
(Who would expect a share) will trust such parcels:
In the third square, the very street and sign
Where the commodity dwells, and does but wait      95
To be delivered, be it pepper, soap,
Hops, or tobacco, oatmeal, woad,° or cheeses.      *blue dye*
All which you may so handle to enjoy,
To your own use, and never stand obliged.
KASTRIL.  I'faith! Is he such a fellow?      100
FACE.                Why, Nab here knows him.
And then for making matches, for rich widows,
Young gentlewomen, heirs, the fortunat'st man!
He's sent to, far and near, all over England,
To have his counsel, and to know their fortunes.
KASTRIL.  God's will, my suster° shall see him.      *sister* 105
FACE.                      I'll tell you, sir,
What he did tell me of Nab. It's a strange thing!
(By the way, you must eat no cheese, Nab, it breeds melancholy:
And that same melancholy breeds worms, but pass it.°)      *forget it*
He told me, honest Nab here was ne'er at tavern,
But once in's life!      110
DRUGGER.        Truth, and no more I was not.

---

1  *perspective*  A trick glass or cleverly distorted painting seen aright only from an odd angle.
Cf. *Richard II* 2.2.16–20.

FACE. And then he was so sick—

DRUGGER.                      Could he tell you that, too?

FACE. How should I know it?

DRUGGER.                   In troth we had been a-shooting,
   And had a piece of fat ram-mutton, to supper,
   That lay so heavy o' my stomach—

FACE.                      And he has no head

115   To bear any wine; for, what with the noise o' the fiddlers,
   And care of his shop, for he dares keep no servants—

DRUGGER. My head did so ache—

FACE.                  And he was fain to be brought home,
   The Doctor told me. And then, a good old woman—

DRUGGER. Yes, faith, she dwells in Seacoal Lane,[1] did cure me

120   With sodden° ale and pellitory° o' the wall.          *boiled* / *herb*
   Cost me but twopence. I had another sickness,
   Was worse than that.

FACE.              Aye, that was with the grief
   Thou took'st for being 'sessed° at eighteen pence,         *taxed*
   For the waterwork.°                    *London pump-house*

DRUGGER.           In truth, and it was like

125   T' have cost me almost my life.

FACE.                Thy hair went off?[2]

DRUGGER. Yes, sir; 'twas done for spite.

FACE.                  Nay, so says the Doctor.

KASTRIL. Pray thee, tobacco-boy, go fetch my suster;
   I'll see this learnèd boy before I go:
   And so shall she.

FACE.        Sir, he is busy now:

130   But if you have a sister to fetch hither,
   Perhaps, your own pains may command her sooner;
   And he, by that time, will be free.

KASTRIL.               I go.            [*Exit.*]

FACE. Drugger, she's thine: the damask! [*Exit Drugger.*]
                                        (Subtle and I
   Must wrestle for her.) Come on, master Dapper.

---

1  *Seacoal Lane*  Impoverished London district.
2  *Thy hair went off*  Symptom of syphilis.

You see how I turn clients here away                    135
To give your cause dispatch. Ha' you performed
The ceremonies were enjoined you?
DAPPER.                              Yes, o' the vinegar,
And the clean shirt.
FACE.                    'Tis well: that shirt may do you
More worship than you think. Your aunt's a-fire,
But that she will not show it, t' have a sight on you.        140
Ha' you provided for her Grace's servants?
DAPPER. Yes, here are six score Edward shillings.[1]
FACE.                                        Good.
DAPPER. And an old Harry's° sovereign.                    *Henry VIII*
FACE.                              Very good.
DAPPER. And three James shillings, and an Elizabeth groat,[2]
Just twenty nobles.                                        145
FACE.                    O, you are too just.
I would you had had the other noble in Mary's.[3]
DAPPER. I have some Philip and Mary's.[4]
FACE.                              Aye, those same
Are best of all. Where are they? Hark, the doctor.


# ACT 3, SCENE 5

*([Enter] Subtle disguised like a Priest of Fairy.)*

SUBTLE. Is yet her Grace's cousin come?
FACE.                              He is come.
SUBTLE. And is he fasting?
FACE.          Yes.
SUBTLE.                    And hath cried "hum"?

---

1  *Edward shillings*  Coins depicting either Edward III (1312–77) or Edward IV (1442–83);
   an Edward shilling, otherwise known as the Edward shovelboard, bore the face of Edward
   VI (1537–53) and was often used in a game called shovelboard.
2  *James shillings*  Coins depicting James I (1603–25);  *Elizabeth groat*  Coin worth four-
   pence, depicting Elizabeth I (1533–1603).
3  *Mary's*  Coins depicting Mary I (1516–58).
4  *Philip and Mary's*  Coins issued after the marriage of Mary I and King Philip of Spain
   (1554).

FACE.  Thrice, you must answer.
DAPPER.                              Thrice.
SUBTLE.                                        And as oft "buzz"?
FACE.  If you have, say.
DAPPER.                    I have.
SUBTLE.                                      Then, to her coz,
5      Hoping, that he hath vinegared his senses,
       As he was bid, the Fairy Queen dispenses,
       By me, this robe, the petticoat of Fortune;
       Which that he straight put on, she doth importune.
       And though to Fortune near be her petticoat,
10     Yet, nearer is her smock,° the Queen doth note:        *undergarment*
       And, therefore, even of that a piece she hath sent,
       Which, being a child, to wrap him in was rent;
       And prays him, for a scarf he now will wear it,
       (With as much love as then her Grace did tear it)
15     About his eyes, to show he is fortunate.

       (*They blind him with a rag.*)

       And, trusting unto her to make his state,°              *fortune*
       He'll throw away all worldly pelf° about him;           *wealth*
       Which that he will perform, she doth not doubt him.
FACE.  She need not doubt him, sir. Alas, he has nothing,
20     But what he will part withal, as willingly,
       Upon her Grace's word (throw away your purse)
       As she would ask it: (handkerchiefs and all)

       (*He throws away as they bid him.*)

       She cannot bid that thing, but he'll obey.
       [*To Dapper.*] If you have a ring about you, cast it off,
25     Or a silver seal at your wrist: her Grace will send
       Her fairies here to search you, therefore deal
       Directly with her Highness. If they find
       That you conceal a mite, you are undone.

DAPPER. Truly, there's all.
FACE.                    All what?
DAPPER.                              My money, truly.
FACE. Keep nothing, that is transitory about you.                    30
  [*Aside to Subtle.*] Bid Doll play music.

(*Doll enters with a cittern.°*)                    *guitar-like instrument*

[*To Dapper.*]                    Look, the elves are come
To pinch you, if you tell not truth. Advise you.

(*They pinch him.*)

DAPPER. O, I have a paper with a spur-royal° in 't.    *15th-century coin*
FACE.                                        *Ti, ti.*
  They knew't, they say.
SUBTLE.                    *Ti, ti, ti, ti.* He has more yet.
FACE. *Ti, ti-ti-ti.* I' the t'other pocket?                    35
SUBTLE.                              *Titi, titi, titi, titi.*
  They must pinch him, or he will never confess, they say.
DAPPER. Oh, Oh!
FACE.                    Nay, pray you hold. He is her Grace's nephew.
  *Ti, ti, ti?* What care you? Good faith, you shall care.
  Deal plainly, sir, and shame the fairies. Show
  You are an innocent.°                    *guiltless, a fool*  40
DAPPER.                    By this good light, I ha' nothing.
SUBTLE. *Ti, ti, tititota.* He does equivocate,° she says:    *deceive*
  *Ti, ti do ti, ti ti do, ti da.* And swears by the light, when he is blinded.
DAPPER. By this good dark, I ha' nothing but a half-crown[1]
  Of gold, about my wrist, that my love gave me;
  And a leaden heart I wore, sin' she forsook me.                    45

(*Exit Doll.*)

FACE. I thought 'twas something. And would you incur
  Your aunt's displeasure for these trifles? Come,
  I had rather you had thrown away twenty half-crowns.
  You may wear your leaden heart still.
                              How now?

---

1  *half-crown*  Gold coin minted under Henry VIII.

SUBTLE.  What news, Doll?

DOLL.                          Yonder's your knight, Sir Mammon.

FACE.  God's lid, we never thought of him, till now.
Where is he?

DOLL.           Here, hard by. He's at the door.

SUBTLE.  And you are not ready, now? Doll, get his suit.
He must not be sent back.

FACE.                          O, by no means.

55      What shall we do with this same puffin,[1] here,
Now he's o' the spit?

SUBTLE.                  Why, lay him back awhile,
With some device. *Ti, ti ti, ti ti ti.*
                                                Would her Grace speak with me?
I come. Help, Doll.

(*He speaks through the keyhole, the other* [*Mammon*] *knocking.*)

FACE.                    Who's there? Sir Epicure;
My master's i' the way. Please you to walk
60      Three or four turns, but till his back be turn'd,
And I am for you.—Quickly, Doll.

SUBTLE.                                Her Grace
Commends her kindly to you, master Dapper.

DAPPER.  I long to see her Grace.

SUBTLE.                          She now is set
At dinner, in her bed; and she has sent you,
65      From her own private trencher, a dead mouse,
And a piece of gingerbread, to be merry withal,
And stay your stomach, lest you faint with fasting:
Yet if you could hold out, till she saw you (she says)
It would be better for you.

FACE.                          Sir, he shall
70      Hold out, and 'twere this two hours, for her Highness;
I can assure you that. We will not lose
All we ha' done—

SUBTLE.           He must not see, nor speak
To anybody, till then.

FACE.                    For that we'll put, sir,

---

1   *puffin*   Elaborately colored seabird; a prideful person.

A stay° in's mouth.                                                    *gag*
SUBTLE.                    Of what?
FACE.                                    Of gingerbread.
    Make you it fit. He that hath pleased her Grace                    75
    Thus far, shall not now crinkle,¹ for a little.
    Gape sir, and let him fit you.

[*They gag Dapper.*]

SUBTLE. [*Aside.*]                                    Where shall we now
    Bestow him?
DOLL. [*Aside.*]      I' the privy.
SUBTLE. [*To Dapper.*]            Come along, sir,
    I now must show you Fortune's privy² lodgings.
FACE. Are they perfumed? And his bath ready?                           80
SUBTLE.                                            All.
    Only the fumigation's somewhat strong.
FACE. Sir Epicure, I am yours, sir, by and by.

[*Exeunt.*]


ACT 4, SCENE I

([*Enter*] *Face* [*and*] *Mammon.*)

FACE. Oh sir, you're come i' the only, finest time—
MAMMON. Where's master?
FACE.                            Now preparing for projection, sir.
    Your stuff will b' all changed shortly.
MAMMON.                              Into gold?
FACE. To gold and silver, sir.
MAMMON.                        Silver, I care not for.
FACE. Yes, sir, a little to give beggars.                              5
MAMMON.                            Where's the lady?
FACE. At hand, here. I ha' told her such brave things o' you,
    Touching your bounty and your noble spirit—
MAMMON.                                        Hast thou?

---

1   *crinkle*  Waver, turn aside from one's purpose.
2   *privy*  Private, with the pun on toilet.

FACE. As she is almost in her fit to see you.
    But, good sir, no divinity i' your conference,
10  For fear of putting her in rage—
MAMMON.                                      I warrant thee.
FACE. Six men will not hold her down. And then,
    If the old man should hear or see you—
MAMMON.                                      Fear not.
FACE. The very house, sir, would run mad. You know it,
    How scrupulous he is, and violent,
15  'Gainst the least act of sin. Physic,° or mathematics,          *medicine*
    Poetry, state,° or bawdry, as I told you,                       *politics*
    She will endure, and never startle: but
    No word of controversy.
MAMMON.                          I am schooled, good Ulen.
FACE. And you must praise her house, remember that,
20  And her nobility.
MAMMON.              Let me alone:
    No herald, no nor antiquary, Lungs,
    Shall do it better. Go.
FACE. [*Aside.*]            Why, this is yet
    A kind of modern° happiness, to have                            *trite*
    Doll Common for a great lady.

    [*Exit.*]

MAMMON.                              Now, Epicure,
25  Heighten thyself, talk to her all in gold;
    Rain her as many showers, as Jove did drops
    Unto his Danaë:[1] show the god a miser,
    Compared with Mammon. What? The stone will do 't.
    She shall feel gold, taste gold, hear gold, sleep gold:
30  Nay, we will *concumbere*° gold. I will be puissant,            *fornicate*
    And mighty in my talk to her! Here she comes.

    ([*Enter Face with*] *Doll.*)

---

1  *Jove ... Danaë* According to Greek mythology, Acrisius imprisoned his daughter Danaë in
   a room of bronze to ensure she would never conceive a son. Zeus, however, fell in love with
   Danaë and came to her as a shower of gold falling into her lap.

FACE. [*Aside.*] To him, Doll, suckle him. [*Aloud.*] This is the noble
   knight,
   I told your ladyship—
MAMMON.                Madam, with your pardon,
   I kiss your vesture.°                         *clothing*
DOLL.              Sir, I were uncivil
   If I would suffer that; my lip to you, sir.            35
MAMMON. I hope, my lord your brother be in health, lady?
DOLL. My lord, my brother is, though I no lady, sir.
FACE. [*Aside.*] Well said, my guinea-bird.°         *prostitute*
MAMMON.                      Right noble madam—
FACE. [*Aside.*] Oh, we shall have most fierce idolatry!
MAMMON. 'Tis your prerogative.                   40
DOLL.                Rather your courtesy.
MAMMON. Were there nought else t'enlarge° your    *declare*
   virtues, to me,
   These answers speak your breeding and your blood.
DOLL. Blood we boast none, sir, a poor Baron's daughter.
MAMMON. Poor! And gat you? Profane not. Had your father
   Slept all the happy remnant of his life             45
   After that act, lien but there still and panted,
   He'd done enough to make himself, his issue,
   And his posterity noble.
DOLL.               Sir, although
   We may be said to want the gilt and trappings,
   The dress of honour, yet we strive to keep         50
   The seeds, and the materials.
MAMMON.              I do see
   The old ingredient, virtue, was not lost,
   Nor the drug, money, used to make your compound.
   There is a strange nobility i' your eye,
   This lip, that chin! Methinks you do resemble     55
   One of the Austriac princes.[1]
FACE. [*Aside.*]             Very like!
   Her father was an Irish costermonger.°        *fruit seller*

---

1  *Austriac princes*  Hapsburg princes were considered to have a large lower lip.

MAMMON. The house of Valois,[1] just, had such a nose.
    And such a forehead, yet, the Medici
60    Of Florence[2] boast.
DOLL.                  Troth, and I have been liken'd
    To all these princes.
FACE. [*Aside.*]          I'll be sworn, I heard it.
MAMMON. I know not how! It is not any one,
    But e'en the very choice of all their features.
FACE. [*Aside.*] I'll in, and laugh.


[*Exit Face.*]


MAMMON.               A certain touch, or air,
65    That sparkles a divinity, beyond
    An earthly beauty!
DOLL.             Oh, you play the courtier.
MAMMON. Good lady, gi' me leave—
DOLL.                   In faith, I may not,
    To mock me, sir.
MAMMON.         To burn i' this sweet flame:
    The phoenix never knew a nobler death.[3]
70 DOLL. Nay, now you court the courtier: and destroy
    What you would build. This art, sir, i' your words,
    Calls your whole faith in question.
MAMMON.            By my soul—
DOLL. Nay, oaths are made o' the same air, sir.
MAMMON.                  Nature
    Never bestowed upon mortality
75    A more unblamed,° a more harmonious feature:°   *unblemished / figure*
    She played the step-dame in all faces else.
    Sweet Madam, le' me be particular—[4]
DOLL. Particular, sir? I pray you, know your distance.
MAMMON. In no ill sense, sweet lady, but to ask
80    How your fair graces pass the hours? I see

---

1   *house of Valois*  Branch of the royal house of France from 1328 to 1589.
2   *Medici of Florence*  Florentine banking family, political dynasty, and royal house.
3   *phoenix ... death*  Mythical bird that is reborn from its own ashes.
4   *particular*  Intimate, familiar.

You're lodged here, i' the house of a rare man,
An excellent artist: but—what's that to you?
DOLL. Yes, sir; I study here the mathematics,
   And distillation.[1]
MAMMON.                O, I cry your pardon.
   He's a divine instructor! Can extract                                85
   The souls of all things, by his art; call all
   The virtues and the miracles of the sun,
   Into a temperate furnace; teach dull nature
   What her own forces are. A man, the Emp'ror
   Has courted, above Kelly:[2] sent his medals                         90
   And chains,[3] t'invite him.
DOLL.                          Ay, and for his physic, sir—
MAMMON. Above the art of Aesculapius,
   That drew the envy of the Thunderer![4]
   I know all this, and more.
DOLL.                          Troth, I am taken, sir,
   Whole, with these studies, that contemplate nature.                  95
MAMMON. It is a noble humour.° But, this form          *inclination*
   Was not intended to so dark a use!
   Had you been crooked, foul, of some coarse mould,
   A cloister had done well: but, such a feature
   That might stand up the glory of a kingdom,                          100
   To live recluse!—is a mere solecism,°                      *error*
   Though in a nunnery. It must not be.
   I muse, my lord your brother will permit it!
   You should spend half my land first, were I he.
   Does not this diamant° better, on my finger,          *diamond*  105

---

1  *mathematics*  I.e., astrology;  *distillation*  Alchemical processes, chemistry.
2  *Kelly*  Sir Edward Kelley (1555–97) was an alchemist and occultist who worked with
   Queen Elizabeth's royal astrologer, Sir John Dee. Kelley convinced Holy Roman Emperor
   Rudolph II in Prague that he was a powerful alchemist, and he lived a life of opulence in
   Prague for some years. The Emperor then wanted Kelley to start making gold with the philosopher's stone; when Kelley refused, Rudolph II imprisoned him from 1591 until 1595,
   until Kelley finally promised to start transmuting metal to gold. His subsequent failure to
   do so led to another imprisonment, during which Kelley eventually died.
3  *chains*  Necklaces, but also, given the reference to Kelley, prison chains.
4  *Aesculapius ... Thunderer*  Asclepius was the Greek god of medicine who incurred the
   wrath of Zeus (the Thunderer) for bringing the dead back to life.

      Than i' the quarry?
DOLL.                  Yes.
MAMMON.                          Why, you are like it.
   You were created, lady, for the light!
   Here, you shall wear it; take it, the first pledge
   Of what I speak: to bind you to believe me.
110 DOLL. In chains of adamant?[1]
MAMMON.                    Yes, the strongest bands.°            bonds
   And take a secret, too. Here, by your side,
   Doth stand, this hour, the happiest man in Europe.
DOLL. You are contented, sir?
MAMMON.                    Nay, in true being:
   The envy of princes and the fear of states.
115 DOLL. Say you so, sir Epicure?
MAMMON.                        Yes, and thou shalt prove it,
   Daughter of honour. I have cast mine eye
   Upon thy form, and I will rear this beauty
   Above all styles.
DOLL.              You mean no treason, sir?
MAMMON. No, I will take away that jealousy.°.            suspicion
120 I am the lord of the philosopher's stone,
   And thou the lady.
DOLL.              How, sir! Ha' you that?
MAMMON. I am the master of the maistry.[2]
   This day, the good old wretch, here, o' the house,
   Has made it for us. Now, he's at projection.
125 Think therefore, thy first wish, now, let me hear it:
   And it shall rain into thy lap, no shower,
   But floods of gold,[3] whole cataracts, a deluge,
   To get a nation on thee!
DOLL.              You are pleased, sir,
   To work on the ambition of our sex.
130 MAMMON. I am pleased the glory of her sex should know,
   This nook, here, of the Friars,° is no climate            Blackfriars
   For her, to live obscurely in, to learn

---

1   *adamant*   Stone of extraordinary hardness, often refers to diamond.
2   *maistry*   Magisterium, i.e., the philosopher's stone.
3   *rain ... gold*   Cf., 2.1 note 10.

Physic, and surgery, for the Constable's wife
Of some odd hundred[1] in Essex; but come forth,
And taste the air of palaces; eat, drink                    135
The toils of emp'rics,[2] and their boasted practice;
Tincture of pearl, and coral, gold, and amber;
Be seen at feasts, and triumphs; have it asked,
What miracle she is? Set all the eyes
Of court a-fire, like a burning-glass,                      140
And work 'em into cinders; when the jewels
Of twenty states adorn thee, and the light
Strikes out the stars; that, when thy name is mentioned,
Queens may look pale: and, we but showing our love,
Nero's Poppaea[3] may be lost in story!                     145
Thus, will we have it.
DOLL.                I could well consent, sir.
But, in a monarchy, how will this be?
The Prince will soon take notice; and both seize
You, and your stone: it being a wealth unfit
For any private subject.                                    150
MAMMON.              If he knew it.
DOLL. Yourself do boast it, sir.
MAMMON.              To thee, my life.
DOLL. O, but beware, sir! You may come to end
The remnant of your days, in a loath'd prison,
By speaking of it.
MAMMON.        'Tis no idle fear!
We'll therefore go with all,° my girl, and live       *our wealth*  155
In a free state;° where we will eat our mullets,°    *republic / fishes*
Soused in high-country wines, sup pheasants' eggs,
And have our cockles,° boiled in silver shells,              *mussels*
Our shrimps to swim again, as when they lived,
In a rare butter, made of dolphins' milk,                    160
Whose cream does look like opals: and with these

---

1   *hundred*   District, part of a county.
2   *emp'rics*   Physicians who value experience over formal training. Their remedies often
    included tinctures of precious metals, pearl, amber, etc.
3   *Nero's Poppaea*   Nero was Emperor of Rome from 37–68 CE. Poppaea was his mistress and
    later wife (after he killed his first wife).

Delicate meats, set ourselves high for pleasure,
And take us down° again, and then renew            *go to bed*
Our youth and strength, with drinking the elixir,
165   And so enjoy a perpetuity
Of life, and lust. And thou shalt ha' thy wardrobe,
Richer than Nature's still, to change thyself,
And vary oft'ner, for thy pride, than she:°         *Nature*
Or Art, her wise, and almost-equal servant.

[*Enter Face.*]

170 FACE.   Sir, you are too loud. I hear you, every word,
Into the laboratory. Some fitter place.
The garden, or great chamber above. How like you her?
MAMMON.   Excellent, Lungs! There's for thee.

[*Gives him money.*]

FACE.                                   But do you hear?
Good sir, beware, no mention of the Rabbins.°     *Jewish scholars*
175 MAMMON.   We think not on 'em.
FACE.                 O, it is well, sir.

[*Exeunt Doll and Mammon.*]

[*Calling.*] Subtle!

## ACT 4, SCENE 2

([*Enter*] *Subtle.*)

FACE.   Dost thou not laugh?
SUBTLE.                Yes. Are they gone?
FACE.                           All's clear.
SUBTLE.   The widow is come.
FACE.                     And your quarrelling disciple?

SUBTLE.  Aye.

FACE.            I must to my captainship¹ again then.

SUBTLE.  Stay, bring 'em in first.

FACE.                          So I meant. What is she?
  A bonnibel?°                                                    *beauty*  5

SUBTLE.            I know not.

FACE.                          We'll draw lots,
  You'll stand to that?

SUBTLE.            What else?

FACE.                          Oh, for a suit,°    *captain's uniform*
  To fall now like a curtain: flap.

SUBTLE.                          To th' door, man.

FACE.  You'll have the first kiss, 'cause I am not ready.

SUBTLE.  [*Aside.*] Yes, and perhaps hit you through both the nostrils.²


([*Enter*] *Kastril* [*and*] *Dame Pliant.*)


FACE.  Who would you speak with?                              10

KASTRIL.                          Where's the Captain?

FACE.                                          Gone, sir,
  About some business.

KASTRIL.            Gone?

FACE.                          He'll return straight.
  But master Doctor, his lieutenant, is here. [*Exit.*]

SUBTLE.  Come near, my worshipful boy, my *terrae fili*,³
  That is, my boy of land; make thy approaches:
  Welcome, I know thy lusts,° and thy desires,          *appetites*  15
  And I will serve and satisfy 'em. Begin,
  Charge me from thence, or thence, or in this line;
  Here is my centre; ground thy quarrel.

KASTRIL.                          You lie.

SUBTLE.  How, child of wrath and anger! The loud lie?
  For what, my sudden boy?                                    20

KASTRIL.            Nay, that look you to,

---

1  *captainship*  His captain's disguise.
2  *hit ... nostrils*  Put your nose out of joint.
3  *terrae fili*  "Son of earth" (Latin), meaning a person with obscure lineage. In alchemy, *terrae fili* were spirits who read signs from handfuls of dirt thrown on the ground.

I am aforehand.[1]

SUBTLE.                O, this's no true grammar,
And as ill logic! You must render causes, child,
Your first and second intentions, know your canons,°                    *rules*
And your divisions, moods, degrees, and differences,
25  Your predicaments,° substance, and accident,                    *assertions*
Series extern, and intern, with their causes
Efficient, material, formal, final,[2]
And ha' your elements perfect—
KASTRIL.                    What is this?
The angry tongue he talks in?
SUBTLE.                    That false precept,
30  Of being aforehand, has deceiv'd a number;
And made 'em enter quarrels, oftentimes,
Before they were aware and, afterward,
Against their wills.
KASTRIL.              How must I do then, sir?
SUBTLE.  I cry this lady mercy. She should, first,
35  Have been saluted. I do call you lady,
Because you are to be one, ere 't be long,
My soft and buxom widow.                    (*He kisses her.*)
KASTRIL.                    Is she, i' faith?
SUBTLE.  Yes, or my art is an egregious liar.
KASTRIL.  How know you?
SUBTLE.                    By inspection, on her forehead,
40  And subtlety[3] of her lip, which must be tasted
Often, to make a judgment.                    (*He kisses her again.*)
                              'Slight, she melts
Like a myrobolane![4] Here is, yet, a line
*In rivo frontis*,[5] tells me, he is no knight.

---

1  *aforehand*  Made the first move.
2  *substance ... accident ... Efficient, material, formal, final*  Aristotelian metaphysics provides
   the basis for this scholarly jargon.
3  *subtlety*  Fine and skillfully made, with a pun on *subtlety* as it is used in cookery, where it
   means an elaborate sugar confection.
4  *myrobolane*  Tropical fruit, plum-like.
5  *In rivo frontis*  Latin: in the frontal vein.

DAME PLIANT. What is he then, sir?

SUBTLE. Let me see your hand.

O, your *linea Fortunae*[1] makes it plain;         45

And *stella,* here, *in monte Veneris:*[2]

But, most of all, *junctura annularis.*°       *ring finger joint*

He is a soldier, or a man of art, lady:

But shall have some great honour shortly.

DAME PLIANT.               Brother,

He's a rare man, believe me!               50

KASTRIL.            Hold your peace.


[*Enter Face.*]


Here comes the t'other rare man. Save you, Captain.

FACE. Good master Kastril. Is this your sister?

KASTRIL.                   Aye, sir.

Please you to kuss her, and be proud to know her?

FACE. I shall be proud to know you, lady.

DAME PLIANT.               Brother,

He calls me lady, too.                     55

KASTRIL.        Aye, peace. I heard it.

FACE. [*Aside.*] The Count is come.

SUBTLE. [*Aside.*]            Where is he?

FACE. [*Aside.*]               At the door.

SUBTLE. [*Aside.*] Why, you must entertain him.

FACE. [*Aside.*]              What'll you do

With these the while?

SUBTLE. [*Aside.*]       Why, have 'em up, and show 'em

Some fustian[3] book, or the dark glass.°         *crystal ball*

FACE. [*Aside.*]           'Fore God,

She is a delicate dabchick![4] I must have her.      60

                                    [*Exit.*]

---

1   *linea Fortunae*   Latin: line of Fortune (in palmistry).

2   *stella ... in monte Veneris*   Latin: star on the mount of Venus. The mount of Venus in palmistry is on the base of the thumb.

3   *fustian*   Pretentious, filled with jargon.

4   *dabchick*   Small water-bird, used here as an endearment.

SUBTLE. [*Aside.*] Must you? Aye, if your fortune will, you must.
  [*To Kastril.*] Come, sir, the Captain will come to us presently.
  I'll ha' you to my chamber of demonstrations,
  Where I will show you both the grammar, and logic,
65 And rhetoric[1] of quarrelling; my whole method,
  Drawn out in tables: and my instrument,
  That hath the several scale upon 't, shall make you
  Able to quarrel, at a straw's breadth, by moonlight.
  And, lady, I'll have you look in a glass
70 Some half an hour, but to clear your eyesight,
  Against° you see your fortune: which is greater,                *until*
  Than I may judge upon the sudden, trust me.

  [*Exeunt.*]


## ACT 4, SCENE 3

([*Enter*] Face.)


FACE. Where are you, Doctor?
SUBTLE. [*Within.*]            I'll come to you presently.
FACE. I will ha' this same widow, now I ha' seen her,
  On any composition.°                                        *terms*

([*Enter*] Subtle.)


SUBTLE.            What do you say?
FACE. Ha' you disposed of them?
SUBTLE.                    I ha' sent 'em up.
5 FACE. Subtle, in troth, I needs must have this widow.
SUBTLE. Is that the matter?
FACE.                Nay, but hear me.
SUBTLE.                            Go to,
  If you rebel once, Doll shall know it all.
  Therefore, be quiet, and obey your chance.

---

1  *grammar ... logic ... rhetoric*  The Trivium or traditional components of education.

FACE. Nay, thou art so violent now—do but conceive:
    Thou art old, and canst not serve—°               *have sex*  10
SUBTLE.                   Who cannot? I?
    'Slight, I will serve her with thee, for a—
FACE.                        Nay,
    But understand: I'll gi' you composition.°        *money*
SUBTLE. I will not treat° with thee: what, sell my fortune?  *bargain*
    'Tis better than my birthright. Do not murmur.
    Win her, and carry her.[1] If you grumble, Doll                15
    Knows it directly.
FACE.            Well, sir, I am silent.
    Will you go help, to fetch in Don, in state?

[*Exit Face.*]

SUBTLE. I follow you, sir: We must keep Face in awe,        20
    Or he will overlook° us like a tyrant.                *dominate*
    Brain of a tailor! Who comes here? Don John![2]

([*Enter*] *Surly like a Spaniard* [*and*] *Face.*)

SURLY.   *Señores, beso las manos a vuestras mercedes.*[3]
SUBTLE. Would you had stoop'd a little, and kiss'd our *anos.*°  *arses*
FACE. Peace, Subtle.
SUBTLE.          Stab me; I shall never hold,° man.  *avoid laughing*  25
    He looks in that deep ruff,[4] like a head in a platter,
    Served in by a short cloak upon two trestles![5]
FACE. Or, what do you say to a collar of brawn, cut down
    Beneath the souse, and wriggled with a knife?[6]
SUBTLE. 'Slud, he does look too fat to be a Spaniard.
FACE. Perhaps some Fleming or some Hollander[7] got° him  *begot*

---

1  *Win her, and carry her*  Whoever wins, takes her ("winner takes all").
2  *Don John*  Common term used to refer to a Spaniard.
3  *Señores ... mercedes*  "Gentlemen, I kiss your honors' hands."
4  *ruff*  Detachable, starched frill of linen worn around the neck.
5  *trestles*  Legs of a table.
6  *collar of brawn*  Meat carved from a pig's neck; *souse* Pig's ear; *wriggled with a knife* Meat cut in a wriggled pattern (similar to the frills of the ruff).
7  *some Fleming or some Hollander*  Someone of Flemish or Dutch origin.

30    In D'Alva's time; Count Egmont's[1] bastard.

SUBTLE.                          Don,

    Your scurvy, yellow, Madrid face is welcome.

SURLY.  *Gracias.°*                          *thank you*

SUBTLE.        He speaks out of a fortification.°    *i.e., the ruff*

    Pray God, he ha' no squibs° in those deep sets.[2]   *explosives*

SURLY.  *Por diós, Señores, muy linda casa!*[3]

35  SUBTLE.  What says he?

FACE.              Praises the house, I think.

    I know no more but's action.

SUBTLE.               Yes, the *casa,*°          *house*

    My precious Diego,[4] will prove fair enough

    To cozen you in. Do you mark? you shall

    Be cozened, Diego.

FACE.              Cozened, do you see,

40  My worthy Donzel,° cozened.          *little Don*

SURLY.               *Entiendo.*°      *I understand*

SUBTLE.  Do you intend it? So do we, dear Don.

    Have you brought pistolets, or portagues?

    My solemn Don?

*(He [Face] feels his pockets.)*

                  Dost thou feel any?

FACE.                   Full.

SUBTLE. You shall be emptied, Don; pumped, and drawn

45  Dry,[5] as they say.

FACE.           Milked, in troth, sweet Don.

SUBTLE.  See all the monsters; the great lion of all, Don.

SURLY.  *Con licencia, se puede ver à està señorà?*[6]

---

1  *D'Alva* Sixteenth-century Governor of the Netherlands; *Egmont* Flemish rebel executed by D'Alva.

2  *sets* Pleats in the ruff.

3  *Por diós ... casa!* "By God, sirs, a very pretty house!"

4  *Diego* Generic, and dismissive, term for a Spaniard; the term "dago," derived from Diego, has been an abusive term for anyone of Spanish or Portugese descent since the early twentieth century.

5  *pumped ... Dry* Financially and sexually.

6  *Con licencia ... señorà?* "If you please, may I see this lady?"

SUBTLE. What talks he now?

FACE.                    O' the *señora*.

SUBTLE.                                   O, Don,
  This is the lioness, which you shall see
  Also, my Don.                                          50

FACE.          'Slid, Subtle, how shall we do?

SUBTLE.  For what?

FACE.            Why, Doll's employed, you know.

SUBTLE.                                      That's true!
  Fore heaven I know not: he must stay,° that's all.          *wait*

FACE.  Stay? That he must not by no means.

SUBTLE.                                No, why?

FACE.  Unless you'll mar all. 'Slight, he'll suspect it.
  And then he will not pay, not half so well.              55
  This is a travell'd punk-master, and does know
  All the delays: a notable hot rascal,
  And looks already rampant.

SUBTLE.                    'Sdeath, and Mammon
  Must not be troubled.

FACE.            Mammon, in no case!

SUBTLE.  What shall we do then?                          60

FACE.                    Think: you must be sudden.

SURLY.  *Entiendo, que la señora es tan hermosa, que codicio tan a verla,*
  *como la bien aventuranza de mi vida.*[1]

FACE.  *Mi vida?* 'Slid, Subtle, he puts me in mind o' the widow.
  What dost thou say to draw her to 't, ha?
  And tell her 'tis her fortune. All our venture          65
  Now lies upon 't. It is but one man more,
  Which on 's[2] chance to have her: and, beside,
  There is no maidenhead, to be feared or lost.
  What dost thou think on 't, Subtle?

SUBTLE.                        Who? I? Why—

FACE.  The credit of our house too is engaged.            70

SUBTLE.  You made me an offer for my share erewhile.

---

1  *Entiendo ... vida*  "I understand the lady is so lovely that I long to see her as the greatest
   good fortune of my life."
2  *Which on 's*  Whichever one of us.

What wilt thou gi' me, i'faith?

FACE.                                         Oh, by that light,
I'll not buy now: You know your doom to me.
E'en take your lot, obey your chance, sir; win her,
75  And wear her—out—for me.

SUBTLE.                    'Slight, I'll not work her[1] then.

FACE.  It is the common cause, therefore bethink you.
Doll else must know it, as you said.

SUBTLE.                                   I care not.

SURLY.  *Señores, por qué se tarda tanto?*[2]

SUBTLE.  Faith, I am not fit, I am old.

FACE.                           That's now no reason, sir.

80  SURLY.  *Puede ser de hazer burla de mi amor?*[3]

FACE.  You hear the Don too? By this air, I call,
And loose the hinges.[4] Doll!

SUBTLE.                         A plague of hell—

FACE.  Will you then do?

SUBTLE.                   You're a terrible rogue,
I'll think of° this: will you, sir, call the widow?                   *remember*

85  FACE.  Yes, and I'll take her too, with all her faults,
Now I do think on 't better.

SUBTLE.                      With all my heart, sir,
Am I discharg'd o' the lot?

FACE.                       As you please.

SUBTLE.                                    Hands.

[*They shake hands.*]

FACE.  Remember now, that upon any change,
You never claim her.

SUBTLE.              Much good joy, and health to you, sir.
90  Marry a whore? Fate, let me wed a witch first.

---

1  *work her*  Work on her (i.e., persuade her to take the Spaniard).
2  *Señores ... tarda tanto?*  "Gentlemen, why so much delay?"
3  *Puede ... mi amor?*  "Perhaps you are making fun of my love?"
4  *loose the hinges*  Weaken our agreement.

SURLY. *Por estas honradas barbas*[1]—
SUBTLE.                           He swears by his beard.
  Dispatch, and call the brother too.

[*Exit Face.*]

SURLY. *Tengo dúda, Señores, que no me hágan alguna traycíon.*[2]
SUBTLE. How, issue on? Yes, *presto, Señor*. Please you
  *Enthratha* the *chambratha*,[3] worthy Don;                              95
  Where if you please the Fates, in your *bathada*,
  You shall be soaked and stroked and tubbed and rubbed
  And scrubbed and fubbed,° dear Don, before you go.          *cheated*
  You shall, in faith, my scurvy baboon Don:
  Be curried, clawed and flawed, and tawed[4] indeed.                    100
  I will the heartilier go about it now,
  And make the widow a punk so much the sooner
  To be revenged on this impetuous Face:
  The quickly doing of it, is the grace.

[*Exeunt.*]


ACT 4, SCENE 4

([*Enter*] *Face, Kastril* [*and*] *Dame Pliant.*)

FACE. Come, lady: I knew the Doctor would not leave,
  Till he had found the very nick° of her fortune.          *precise moment*
KASTRIL. To be a Countess, say you?
FACE.                          A Spanish Countess, sir.
DAME PLIANT. Why, is that better than an English Countess?
FACE. Better? 'Slight, make you that a question, lady?                    5

---

1  *Por ... barbas*  "By this honored beard."
2  *Tengo ... traycíon*  "I suspect, gentlemen, that you are deceiving me."
3  *Enthratha the chambratha*  Fake Spanish for "enter the chamber" (which continues below,
   with "bathada" for "bath").
4  *curried, clawed and flawed, and tawed*  Sequence of curing leather: beaten, scraped, flayed,
   and soaked or softened.

KASTRIL. Nay, she is a fool, Captain, you must pardon her.

FACE. Ask from your courtier, to your inns-of-court-man,°  *lawyer*
 To your mere milliner: they will tell you all,
 Your Spanish gennet° is the best horse. Your Spanish  *small horse*
10 Stoop° is the best garb.° Your Spanish beard  *bow / style*
 Is the best cut. Your Spanish ruffs are the best
 Wear. Your Spanish pavane° the best dance.  *court dance*
 Your Spanish titillation° in a glove  *perfume*
 The best perfume. And, for your Spanish pike,°  *spear*
15 And Spanish blade,° let your poor Captain speak.  *sword*
 Here comes the Doctor.

 ([*Enter*] *Subtle*.)

SUBTLE.     My most honoured lady,
 (For so I am now to style you, having found
 By this my scheme,° you are to undergo  *horoscope*
 An honourable fortune, very shortly.)
20 What will you say now, if some—
FACE.       I ha' told her all, sir,
 And her right worshipful brother, here, that she shall be
 A Countess: do not delay 'em, sir. A Spanish Countess.
SUBTLE. Still, my scarce worshipful Captain, you can keep
 No secret. Well, since he has told you, madam,
25 Do you forgive him, and I do.
KASTRIL.     She shall do that, sir;
 I'll look to 't, 'tis my charge.
SUBTLE.    Well then. Naught rests°  *remains*
 But that she fit her love, now, to her fortune.
DAME PLIANT. Truly, I shall never brook a Spaniard.
SUBTLE.       No?
DAME PLIANT. Never, sin' eighty-eight[1] could I abide 'em,
30 And that was some three year afore I was born, in truth.
SUBTLE. Come, you must love him, or be miserable:

---

1 *eighty-eight* I.e., 1588, the year of the Spanish Armada, when Spain sent a fleet with the aim
 of attacking England and deposing Elizabeth I. The attempt was foiled, securing Elizabeth
 I's rule, but the Spanish were not well-regarded for some time afterwards (though at the time
 *The Alchemist* was written, James I was attempting to build good relations with Spain).

Choose, which you will.

FACE.                    By this good rush,° persuade her,    *floor covering*
She will cry strawberries¹ else, within this twelvemonth.

SUBTLE.  Nay, shads and mackerel,² which is worse.

FACE.                                              Indeed, sir?

KASTRIL.  God's lid, you shall love him, or I'll kick you.          35

DAME PLIANT.                                          Why,
I'll do as you will ha' me, brother.

KASTRIL.                    Do,
Or by this hand, I'll maul you.

FACE.                    Nay, good sir,
Be not so fierce.

SUBTLE.          No, my enragèd child,
She will be ruled. What, when she comes to taste
The pleasures of a Countess! To be courted—                 40

FACE. And kissed, and ruffled!°                    *petted*

SUBTLE.                    Aye, behind the hangings.³

FACE. And then come forth in pomp!

SUBTLE.                    And know her state!°    *status*

FACE. Of keeping all th' idolaters o' the chamber
Barer to her,⁴ than at their prayers!

SUBTLE.                    Is serv'd
Upon the knee!                                              45

FACE.          And has her pages, ushers,
Footmen, and coaches—

SUBTLE.                    Her six mares—

FACE.                              Nay, eight!

SUBTLE. To hurry her through London, to th' Exchange,
Bet'lem, the China-houses⁵—

FACE.                    Yes, and have

---

1  *cry strawberries*  Sell fruit in the street.
2  *shads and mackerel*  Fish-mongers were very poorly regarded. Selling fruit and fish in the street are also suggestive of prostitution.
3  *hangings*  Wall-hangings in the houses of the upper classes provided good hiding places for trysts.
4  *idolaters … to her*  Her admirers would remove their hats to her (bare their heads) more often and more dutifully than they do for prayers.
5  *th' Exchange*  Fashionable meeting place and shops; *Bet'lem*  Bethlehem Royal Hospital for the mentally ill, where fashionable visitors would pay a fee to view the patients; *China-houses*  Shops selling luxury goods from the East.

The citizens gape at her, and praise her tires!°         *clothes*
50 And my lord's goose-turd bands,[1] that rides with her!
KASTRIL. Most brave! By this hand, you are not my suster,
  If you refuse.
DAME PLIANT.   I will not refuse, brother.

([*Enter*] *Surly*.)

SURLY. *Qué es esto, Señores, que no se venga?*
  *Esta tardanza me mata!*[2]
FACE.               It is the Count come!
55 The Doctor knew he would be here, by his art.
SUBTLE. *En gallanta madama, Don! Gallantissima!*[3]
SURLY. *Por todos los dioses, la mas acabada hermosura, que he visto en*
  *mi vida!*[4]
FACE. Is 't not a gallant language that they speak?
KASTRIL. An admirable language! Is 't not French?
60 FACE. No, Spanish, sir.
KASTRIL.            It goes like law-French,[5]
  And that, they say, is the courtliest language.
FACE. List, sir.
SURLY. *El sol ha perdido su lumbre, con el esplandor que trae esta*
  *dama! Válgame diós!*[6]
FACE. He admires your sister.
KASTRIL.              Must not she make curtsy?
65 SUBTLE. Od's will, she must go to him, man; and kiss him!
  It is the Spanish fashion, for the women
  To make first court.
FACE.           'Tis true he tells you, sir:

---

1  *goose-turd bands*   Collars in the fashionable color of "goose-turd green."
2  *Qué es esto, Señores … me mata!*   "Why is it, gentlemen, that she doesn't come? The delay is killing me."
3  *En gallanta, madama … Gallantissima!*   Subtle's fake Spanish again: "A fine madam, Don, very fine!"
4  *Por todos … mi vida!*   "By all the gods the most perfect beauty I have seen in my life!"
5  *law-French*   Norman-French used in English courts until the seventeenth century.
6  *El sol … Válgame diós!*   "The sun has lost his light with the splendor that this lady brings. So help me God!"

His art knows all.

SURLY. *Por qué no se acude?*[1]

KASTRIL. He speaks to her, I think?

FACE. That he does, sir.

SURLY. *Por el amor de diós, qué es esto que se tarda?*[2]                    70

KASTRIL. Nay, see: she will not understand him! Gull!
    Noddy![3]

DAME PLIANT. What say you, brother?

KASTRIL. Ass, my suster,
    Go kuss him, as the cunning man would ha' you;
    I'll thrust a pin i' your buttocks else.

FACE. O no sir.

SURLY. *Señora mia, mi persona esta muy indigna de allegar a tanta*    75
    *hermosura.*[4]

FACE. Does he not use her bravely?

KASTRIL. Bravely, i'faith!

FACE. Nay, he will use her better.

KASTRIL. Do you think so?

SURLY. *Señora, si sera servida, entremos.*[5]

[*Exit Surly and Dame Pliant.*]

KASTRIL. Where does he carry her?

FACE. Into the garden, sir;
    Take you no thought: I must interpret for her.                    80

SUBTLE. [*Aside to Face.*] Give Doll the word.°                    cue

[*Exit Face.*]

Come, my fierce child, advance,
    We'll to our quarrelling lesson again.

KASTRIL. Agreed.
    I love a Spanish boy, with all my heart.

SUBTLE. Nay, and by this means, sir, you shall be brother

---

1  *Por qué no se acude?*  "Why does she not come?"
2  *Por el amor de diós ... que se tarda?*  "For the love of God, why does she hesitate?"
3  *Noddy*  Dark-plumaged tern; also, as with "gull," a fool or simpleton.
4  *Señora mia ... tanta hermosura*  "My lady, my person is unworthy of approaching such
    beauty."
5  *Señora ... entremos*  "Lady, if it please you, let us go in."

85 To a great Count.
KASTRIL.                    Aye, I knew that, at first.
    This match will advance the house of the Kastrils.
SUBTLE. Pray God, your sister prove but Pliant.
KASTRIL.                                        Why,
    Her name is so: by her other husband.
SUBTLE.                            How!
KASTRIL. The widow Pliant. Knew you not that?
SUBTLE.                                    No, faith, sir.
90 Yet, by erection of her figure,¹ I guess'd it.
    Come, let's go practise.
KASTRIL.              Yes, but do you think, Doctor,
    I e'er shall quarrel well?
SUBTLE.            I warrant you.


[*Exeunt.*]


ACT 4, SCENE 5


([*Enter*] *Doll in her fit of talking,*² [*and*] *Mammon.*)


DOLL. For after Alexander's³ death—
MAMMON.                        Good lady—
DOLL. That Perdicas, and Antigonus, were slain,
    The two that stood, Seleuc' and Ptolomy⁴—
MAMMON. Madam.
DOLL.              Made up the two legs, and the fourth Beast.
5  That was Gog-north, and Egypt-south: which after
    Was called Gog Iron-leg and South Iron-leg—
MAMMON.                        Lady—
DOLL. And then Gog-horned. So was Egypt, too.

---

1  *by ... figure* From her horoscope, also "from the way she looks," perhaps also a sexual pun,
   "from the erections her figure incites."
2  *fit of talking* Doll's ravings, until line 32, are drawn from *A Concent of Scripture* (1590) by
   theologian Hugh Broughton (1549–1612).
3  *Alexander's* Alexander the Great, King of Macedon (356–323 BCE).
4  *Perdicas ... Antigonus ... Seleuc' ... Ptolemy* Alexander the Great's four generals; upon his
   death, Alexander divided his empire between them.

Then Egypt clay-leg, and Gog clay-leg—
MAMMON.                                    Sweet madam.
DOLL.  And last Gog-dust, and Egypt-dust, which fall
   In the last link of the fourth chain.[1] And these                    10
   Be stars in story, which none see, or look at—
MAMMON.  What shall I do?
DOLL.                                For, as he says, except
   We call the Rabbins, and the heathen Greeks—
MAMMON.  Dear lady.
DOLL.                    To come from Salem,° and from Athens, *Jerusalem*
   And teach the people of Great Britain—                               15

([*Enter*] *Face*.)


FACE.                                    What's the matter, sir?
DOLL.  To speak the tongue of Eber, and Javan—[2]
MAMMON.                                    Oh,
   She's in her fit.
DOLL.            We shall know nothing—
FACE.                                    Death, sir,
   We are undone.
DOLL.            Where, then, a learned linguist
   Shall see the ancient us'd communion
   Of vowels and consonants—                                            20
FACE.                          My master will hear!
DOLL.  A wisdom, which Pythagoras held most high—
MAMMON.  Sweet honourable lady!
DOLL.                          To comprise
   All sounds of voices, in few marks of letters—
FACE.  Nay, you must never hope to lay[3] her now.

---

1  *fourth chain*  In Broughton's scheme, the fourth period of history, which precedes the
   apocalypse.
2  *Eber*  Hebrew (after the great-grandson of Shem, one of Noah's three sons, ancestor of
   the Hebrews); *Javan*  Greek (son of Japheth, another of Noah's sons, ancestor of the
   Gentiles).
3  *lay*  Quiet down; also, "get her to bed."

(*They speak together.*)

25 DOLL. And so we may arrive by Talmud[1] skill,
And profane Greek, to raise the building up,
Of Helen's house,[2] against the Ismaelite,
King of Thogarma,[3] and his Habergions[4]
Brimstony, blue, and fiery; and the force
30 Of king Abaddon, and the Beast of Cittim:[5]
Which Rabbi David Kim-chi, Onkelos,[6]
And Aben-Ezra[7] do interpret Rome.

FACE. How did you put her into 't?
MAMMON.    Alas, I talk'd
Of a fifth monarchy I would erect,
With the philosopher's stone (by chance) and she
Falls on the other four straight.
FACE.        Out of Broughton!
I told you so. 'Slid, stop her mouth.
MAMMON.    Is't best?
FACE. She'll never leave else. If the old man hear her,
We are but faeces, ashes.
SUBTLE. (*Within.*)    What's to do there?
FACE. O, we are lost. Now she hears him, she is quiet.

(*Upon Subtle's entry they disperse.*)

[*Exeunt Face and Doll.*]

---

1  *Talmud*  Jewish biblical commentary on the Torah or law.

2  *Helen's house*  I.e., the Kingdom of God; in Broughton, this should read "Heber's" but Doll is mixing her Greek and Hebrew.

3  *Thogarma*  In Genesis 10, the Thogarmah are a people recognized by the Hebrews as having descended from Noah.

4  *Habergions*  Armor of the four horsemen of the apocalypse in Wyclif's English translation of *Revelation* 9.17 in the Latin Bible.

5  *Abaddon ... Cittim*  In Broughton, these are names used for the Pope.

6  *Rabbi David Kimchi*  Jewish biblical scholar (1160–1235); *Onkelos*  First-century translator of the Old Testament into Aramaic.

7  *Aben-Ezra*  Eleventh-century poet and biblical scholar who brought Arab learning to the Europeans.

MAMMON. Where shall I hide me?
SUBTLE.                          How! What sight is here!
  Close° deeds of darkness, and that shun the light!     *secret*
  Bring him again.° Who is he? What, my son!     *back* 35
  Oh, I have lived too long.
MAMMON.                    Nay, good, dear father,
  There was no unchaste purpose.
SUBTLE.                          Not? And flee me,
  When I come in?
MAMMON.        That was my error.
SUBTLE.                        Error?
  Guilt, guilt, my son. Give it the right name. No marvel,
  If I found check in our great work within,     40
  When such affairs as these were managing!°     *happening*
MAMMON. Why, have you so?
SUBTLE.                It has stood still this half-hour:
  And all the rest of our less works gone back.
  Where is the instrument of wickedness,
  My lewd false drudge?     45
MAMMON.              Nay, good sir, blame not him.
  Believe me, 'twas against his will, or knowledge.
  I saw her by chance.
SUBTLE.              Will you commit more sin,
  T' excuse a varlet?
MAMMON.          By my hope, 'tis true, sir.
SUBTLE. Nay, then I wonder less, if you, for whom
  The blessing was prepar'd, would so tempt heaven:     50
  And lose your fortunes.
MAMMON.              Why, sir?
SUBTLE.                          This'll retard
  The work, a month at least.
MAMMON.                  Why, if it do,
  What remedy? But think it not, good father:
  Our purposes were honest.°     *chaste*
SUBTLE.                    As they were,
  So the reward will prove.     55

(*A great crack and noise within.*)

How now! Aye me.

God, and all saints be good to us. What's that?

[*Enter Face.*]

FACE.  O, sir, we are defeated! All the works
Are flown *in fumo*,° every glass is burst.                           *in smoke*
Furnace, and all rent down! As if a bolt
60    Of thunder had been driven through the house.
Retorts, receivers, pelicans, bolt-heads,
All struck in shivers!°                                                  *splinters*

(*Subtle falls down as in a swoon.*)

                              Help, good sir! Alas,
Coldness, and death invades him. Nay, Sir Mammon,
Do the fair offices of a man! You stand,
65    As you were readier to depart, than he.

(*One knocks.*)

Who's there? [*Looking out.*] My lord her brother is come.
MAMMON.                                              Ha, Lungs?
FACE.  His coach is at the door. Avoid his sight,
For he's as furious° as his sister is mad.                         *hot-tempered*
MAMMON.  Alas!
FACE.              My brain is quite undone with the fume, sir,
70    I ne'er must hope to be mine own man again.
MAMMON.  Is all lost, Lungs? Will nothing be preserved
Of all our cost?
FACE.              Faith, very little, sir;
A peck of coals, or so, which is cold comfort, sir.
MAMMON.  O, my voluptuous mind! I am justly punished.
75 FACE.  And so am I, sir.
MAMMON.              Cast from all my hopes—
FACE.  Nay, certainties, sir.
MAMMON.                  By mine own base affections.

(*Subtle seems come to himself.*)

SUBTLE.  O, the curst fruits of vice, and lust!
MAMMON.                                              Good father,

It was my sin. Forgive it.

SUBTLE.                  Hangs my roof
    Over us still, and will not fall, O justice,
    Upon us, for this wicked man!                  80

FACE.                      Nay, look, sir,
    You grieve him, now, with staying in his sight:
    Good sir, the nobleman will come too, and take you,
    And that may breed a tragedy.

MAMMON.               I'll go.

FACE. Aye, and repent at home, sir. It may be,
    For some good penance you may ha' it yet,         85
    A hundred pound to the box at Bet'lem—

MAMMON.                      Yes.

FACE. For the restoring such as ha' their wits.

MAMMON.                  I'll do't.

FACE. I'll send one to you to receive it.

MAMMON.               Do.
    Is no projection left?

FACE.             All flown, or stinks, sir.

MAMMON. Will nought be saved, that's good for med'cine, think'st  90
    thou?

FACE. I cannot tell, sir. There will be, perhaps,
    Something, about the scraping of the shards,
    Will cure the itch: [*Aside.*] though not your itch of mind, sir.
    [*Aloud.*] It shall be saved for you, and sent home. Good sir,
    This way: for fear the lord should meet you.         95

[*Exit Mammon.*]

SUBTLE.                         Face!

FACE. Aye.

SUBTLE.    Is he gone?

FACE.                Yes, and as heavily
    As all the gold he hoped for, were in his blood.
    Let us be light, though.

SUBTLE.              Aye, as balls, and bound
    And hit our heads against the roof for joy:
    There's so much of our care now cast away.        100

FACE. Now to our Don.

SUBTLE.                              Yes, your young widow, by this time,
   Is made a Countess, Face: she has been in travail[1]
   Of a young heir for you.

FACE.                         Good, sir.

105 SUBTLE.                                 Off with your case,°     *costume*
   And greet her kindly, as a bridegroom should,
   After these common hazards.

FACE.                            Very well, sir.
   Will you go fetch Don Diego off, the while?

SUBTLE. And fetch him over[2] too, if you'll be pleased, sir:

110 Would Doll were in her place, to pick his pockets now.

FACE. Why, you can do it as well, if you would set to 't.
   I pray you prove your virtue.

SUBTLE.                              For your sake, sir.

[*Exeunt.*]


## ACT 4, SCENE 6

([*Enter*] Surly [*and*] Dame Pliant.)

SURLY. Lady, you see into what hands you are fall'n;
   'Mongst what a nest of villains! And how near
   Your honour was t' have catched a certain clap,[3]
   Through your credulity, had I but been
5  So punctually forward, as place, time,
   And other circumstances would ha' made a man:
   For y' are a handsome woman: would y' were wise, too.
   I am a gentleman come here disguised,
   Only to find the knaveries of this citadel,
10 And where I might have wronged your honour, and have not,
   I claim some interest in your love. You are,
   They say, a widow, rich: and I am a bachelor,
   Worth nought. Your fortunes may make me a man,

---

1  *in travail*  Exerting herself.
2  *fetch him over*  Get the better of him or take advantage of him.
3  *clap*  Suffer unworthy treatment or misfortune; also, as it is today, a colloquialism for
   gonorrhoea.

As mine ha' preserved you a woman. Think upon it,
And whether I have deserved you, or no.                                     15
DAME PLIANT.                                        I will, sir.
SURLY.  And for these household-rogues, let me alone
    To treat with them.

([*Enter*] *Subtle*.)

SUBTLE.                    How doth my noble Diego?
    And my dear Madam Countess? Hath the Count
    Been courteous, lady? Liberal? And open?
    Donzel, methinks you look melancholic,                                  20
    After your *coitum*, and scurvy! Truly,
    I do not like the dulness of your eye:
    It hath a heavy cast, 'tis upsee Dutch,[1]
    And says you are a lumpish° whoremaster.                        *dull*
    Be lighter, and I will make your pockets so.                            25

(*He falls to picking of them.*)

SURLY.  Will you, Don bawd and pickpurse? (*Revealing himself.*)
    How now? Reel you?
    Stand up sir, you shall find since I am so heavy,
    I'll gi' you equal weight.
SUBTLE.                        Help, murder!
SURLY.                                        No, sir.
    There's no such thing intended. A good cart,
    And a clean whip[2] shall ease you of that fear.                       30
    I am the Spanish Don, that should be cozened,
    Do you see? Cozened? Where's your Captain Face?
    That parcel-broker,° and whole-bawd, all rascal.            *go-between*

([*Enter*] *Face*.)

---

1  *upsee Dutch*  Like the Dutch.
2  *cart ... whip*  The public punishment for bawds, pimps, and prostitutes was to be whipped
    while being dragged through the streets behind a cart.

FACE. How, Surly!

SURLY.                    O, make your approach, good Captain.
35    I've found, from whence your copper rings,[1] and spoons
      Come, now, wherewith you cheat abroad in taverns.
      'Twas here, you learned t'anoint your boot with brimstone,
      Then rub men's gold on't[2] for a kind of touch,°                          *test*
      And say 'twas naught, when you had changed the colour,
40    That you might ha't for nothing! And this Doctor,
      Your sooty, smoky-bearded compeer, he
      Will close you so much gold in a bolt's-head,
      And, on a turn, convey, i' the stead, another
      With sublim'd mercury, that shall burst i' the heat,
45    And fly out all *in fumo*![3] Then weeps Mammon:
      Then swoons his worship.

      [*Exit Face.*]

                         Or, he is the Faustus,[4]
      That casteth figures and can conjure, cures
      Plagues, piles, and pox, by the ephemerides,°      *astronomical almanacs*
      And holds intelligence with all the bawds
50    And midwives of three shires! While you send in—
      Captain! (what, is he gone?)—damsels with child,
      Wives, that are barren, or the waiting-maid
      With the green sickness!° Nay, sir, you must tarry      *anemia*
      Though he be scaped; and answer, by the ears, sir.

                         ACT 4, SCENE 7

      ([*Enter*] Face [*and*] Kastril.)

FACE. Why, now's the time, if ever you will quarrel
      Well (as they say) and be a true-born child.°          *knight errant*

---

1  *copper rings* Treated to look like gold.
2  *anoint your boot … rub men's gold on't* Brimstone on a boot would serve to blacken gold
   when rubbed against it to make it look impure and therefore cheap.
3  *fly out all in fumo* Refined ("sublim'd" or sublimated) mercury replaces gold in a flask
   heated until it explodes, allowing the trickster to claim that the gold had been lost in a failed
   experiment.
4  *Faustus* Legendary 16th-century German magician made famous by Christopher Mar-
   lowe's (1564–1593) play *Doctor Faustus* (published 1604).

The Doctor, and your sister, both are abus'd.

KASTRIL. Where is he? Which is he? He is a slave
  Whate'er he is, and the son of a whore. [*To Surly.*] Are you          5
  The man, sir, I would know?

SURLY.                                    I should be loth, sir,
  To confess so much.

KASTRIL.            Then you lie, i' your throat.[1]

SURLY.                                          How?

FACE. A very arrant° rogue, sir, and a cheater,                          *errant*
  Employed here by another conjurer,
  That does not love the Doctor, and would cross him,                    10
  If he knew how—

SURLY.          Sir, you are abused.

KASTRIL.                          You lie:
  And 'tis no matter.

FACE.            Well said, sir! He is
  The impudent'st rascal—

SURLY.              You are indeed. Will you hear me, sir?

FACE. By no means. Bid him be gone.

KASTRIL.                        Begone, sir, quickly.

SURLY. This's strange! Lady, do you inform your brother.                 15

FACE. There is not such a foist° in all the town.                       *cheater*
  The Doctor had him, presently;[2] and finds, yet,
  The Spanish Count will come here.
  [*Aside to Subtle.*]              Bear up,° Subtle.        *help me*

SUBTLE. Yes, sir, he must appear within this hour.

FACE. And yet this rogue would come, in a disguise,
  By the temptation of another spirit,                                   20
  To trouble our art, though he could not hurt it.

KASTRIL.                                    Aye,
  I know—[*To Dame Pliant.*] Away, you talk like a foolish
  mauther.°                                                              *girl*

[*Exit Dame Pliant.*]

SURLY. Sir, all is truth she says.

FACE.                  Do not believe him, sir.

---

1  *lie, i' your throat*  The lie direct; Kastril uses the most serious argumentative challenge right away.
2  *had him, presently*  Saw through him right away.

25  He is the lying'st swabber![1] Come your ways, sir.
SURLY.  You are valiant, out of company.[2]
KASTRIL.                                   Yes, how then, sir?

([*Enter*] *Drugger*.)

FACE.  Nay, here's an honest fellow too, that knows him,
    And all his tricks. (Make good what I say, Abel,
    This cheater would ha' cozened thee o' the widow.)
30  He owes this honest Drugger, here, seven pound,
    He has had on him in twopenny'orths of tobacco.
DRUGGER.  Yes, sir. And he's damned himself three terms[3] to pay me.
FACE.  And what does he owe for lotium?[4]
DRUGGER.                               Thirty shillings, sir;
    And for six syringes.
SURLY.                    Hydra[5] of villainy!
35 FACE.  Nay, sir, you must quarrel him out o' the house.
KASTRIL.                                         I will.
    Sir, if you get not out o' doors, you lie:
    And you are a pimp.
SURLY.                  Why, this is madness, sir,
    Not valour in you: I must laugh at this.
KASTRIL.  It is my humour: you are a pimp and a trig,[6]
40  And an Amadis de Gaul, or a Don Quixote.[7]
DRUGGER.  Or a Knight o' the Curious Coxcomb. Do you see?

([*Enter*] *Ananias*.)

ANANIAS.  Peace to the household.
KASTRIL.                          I'll keep peace for no man.
ANANIAS.  Casting of dollars is concluded lawful.

---

1  *swabber*  Lowest rank of sailor.
2  *out of company*  When others are around to help you.
3  *three terms*  Three law terms.
4  *lotium*  Stale urine for hairdressing.
5  *Hydra*  Multi-headed monster of Greek mythology whose heads regrow when cut off; it
   was the second labor of Hercules to kill the Hydra.
6  *humour*  Inclination;  *trig*  Affected person.
7  *Amadis ... Quixote*  Heroes of Spanish romances.

KASTRIL.  Is he the Constable?
SUBTLE.                    Peace, Ananias.
FACE.                            No, sir.
KASTRIL.  Then you are an otter, and a shad, a whit,               45
  A very tim.¹
SURLY.         You'll hear me, sir?
KASTRIL.                        I will not.
ANANIAS.  What is the motive?
SUBTLE.                    Zeal, in the young gentleman,
  Against his Spanish slops—
ANANIAS.                    They are profane,
  Lewd, superstitious, and idolatrous breeches.
SURLY.  New rascals!                                               50
KASTRIL.         Will you begone, sir?
ANANIAS.                        Avoid, Satan,
  Thou art not of the light. That ruff of pride
  About thy neck, betrays thee; and is the same
  With that, which the unclean birds, in seventy-seven,²
  Were seen to prank it° with, on divers coasts.            *play tricks*
  Thou look'st like Antichrist, in that lewd hat.            55
SURLY.  I must give way.
KASTRIL.             Begone, sir.
SURLY.                        But I'll take
  A course with you—
ANANIAS.             Depart, proud Spanish fiend,
SURLY.  Captain and Doctor—
ANANIAS.                    Child of perdition.
KASTRIL.                              Hence, sir.

[*Exit Surly.*]

  Did I not quarrel bravely?
FACE.                    Yes, indeed, sir.
KASTRIL.  Nay, and I give my mind to 't, I shall do 't.           60

---

1  *otter ... shad ... whit ... tim*  Terms of contempt.
2  *unclean birds, in seventy-seven*  Unclean birds are one of a myriad of signs of the Last Judgment and the predicted fall of Babylon in *Revelation* 18.2. Seventy-seven is an unknown reference.

FACE. O, you must follow, sir, and threaten him tame.
    He'll turn° again else.                              *return*
KASTRIL.           I'll re-turn him then.

[*Exit.*]

[*Subtle takes Ananias aside.*]

FACE. Drugger, this rogue prevented° us, for thee:     *forestalled*
    We had determined, that thou should'st ha' come
65   In a Spanish suit, and ha' carried her so; and he,
    A brokerly slave, goes, puts it on himself.
    Hast brought the damask?
DRUGGER.              Yes, sir.
FACE.                  Thou must borrow
    A Spanish suit. Hast thou no credit with the players?
DRUGGER. Yes, sir, did you never see me play the fool?
70 FACE. I know not, Nab: [*Aside.*] Thou shalt, if I can help it.
    Hieronimo's[1] old cloak, ruff, and hat will serve,
    I'll tell thee more, when thou bring'st 'em.

[*Exit Drugger.*]

(*Subtle hath whispered with him [Ananias] this while.*)

ANANIAS.                  Sir, I know
    The Spaniard hates the brethren, and hath spies
    Upon their actions: and that this was one
75   I make no scruple. But the holy synod°       *puritan assembly*
    Have been in prayer, and meditation, for it.
    And 'tis revealed no less, to them, than me,
    That casting of money is most lawful.
SUBTLE.                 True,
    But here, I cannot do it; if the house
80   Should chance to be suspected, all would out,

---

1  *Hieronimo*  Hamlet-like hero of *The Spanish Tragedy*, a popular Elizabethan play by Thomas
  Kyd.

And we be locked up in the Tower, for ever,
To make gold there (for th' state), never come out:
And then are you defeated.
ANANIAS.                                    I will tell
This to the elders, and the weaker brethren,
That the whole company of the separation¹                        85
May join in humble prayer again.
SUBTLE.                                    And fasting.
ANANIAS. Yea, for some fitter place. The peace of mind
Rest with these walls.
SUBTLE.                        Thanks, courteous Ananias.

[*Exit Ananias.*]

FACE. What did he come for?
SUBTLE.                                    About casting dollars,
Presently, out of hand. And so I told him,                        90
A Spanish minister came here to spy,
Against the faithful—
FACE.                        I conceive.° Come, Subtle,        *understand*
Thou art so down upon the least disaster!
How wouldst th' ha' done, if I had not help'd thee out?
SUBTLE. I thank thee, Face, for the angry boy, i' faith.        95
FACE. Who would ha' look'd it should ha' been that rascal?
Surly? He had dy'd his beard, and all. Well, sir,
Here's damask come to make you a suit.
SUBTLE.                                    Where's Drugger?
FACE. He is gone to borrow me a Spanish habit,
I'll be the Count now.                                        100
SUBTLE.                        But where's the widow?
FACE. Within, with my lord's sister: Madam Doll
Is entertaining her.
SUBTLE.                        By your favour, Face,
Now she is honest, I will stand again.
FACE. You will not offer it?
SUBTLE.                        Why?
FACE.                                    Stand to your word,

---

1   *separation* Cf. 3.1.2.

105    Or—here comes Doll. She knows—

SUBTLE.                   You're tyrannous still.

FACE.  Strict for my right.

([*Enter*] *Doll.*)

                    How now, Doll? Hast' told her,
  The Spanish count will come?

DOLL.             Yes, but another is come,
  You little look'd for!

FACE.          Who's that?

DOLL.              Your master:
  The master of the house.

SUBTLE.        How, Doll!

FACE.               She lies.

110  This is some trick. Come, leave your quiblins,° Dorothy.   *quibbles*

DOLL.  Look out, and see.

SUBTLE.        Art thou in earnest?

DOLL.               'Slight,
  Forty o' the neighbours are about him, talking.

FACE.  [*Looking out.*] 'Tis he, by this good day.

DOLL.              'Twill prove ill day
  For some on us.

FACE.        We are undone, and taken.°     *caught*

115 DOLL.  Lost, I'm afraid.

SUBTLE.       You said he would not come,
  While there died one a week, within the liberties.°  *suburbs*

FACE.  No: 'twas within the walls.[1]

SUBTLE.          Was't so? Cry you mercy:
  I thought the liberties. What shall we do now, Face?

FACE.  Be silent: not a word, if he call, or knock.

120  I'll into mine old shape° again, and meet him,     *costume*
  Of Jeremy, the butler. I' the meantime,
  Do you two pack up all the goods, and purchase,°  *winnings*
  That we can carry i' the two trunks. I'll keep him
  Off for today, if I cannot longer: and then

125  At night, I'll ship you both away to Ratcliff,[2]

---

1  *within the walls* Of the city.

2  *Ratcliff* A village downriver from London.

Where we will meet tomorrow, and there we'll share.
Let Mammon's brass, and pewter, keep° the cellar:        *stay in*
We'll have another time for that. But, Doll,
'Pray thee go heat a little water, quickly,
Subtle must shave me. All my Captain's beard                      130
Must off, to make me appear smooth Jeremy.
You'll do it?
SUBTLE.        Yes, I'll shave you, as well as I can.
FACE. And not cut my throat, but trim¹ me?
SUBTLE.                                        You shall see, sir.

[*Exeunt.*]


ACT 5, SCENE I

([*Enter*] *Lovewit* [*and*] *Neighbours.*)

LOVEWIT. Has there been such resort,° say you?        *coming and going*
NEIGHBOUR 1.                                        Daily, sir.
NEIGHBOUR 2. And nightly, too.
NEIGHBOUR 3.                        Aye, some as brave° as lords.  *finely dressed*
NEIGHBOUR 4. Ladies and gentlewomen.
NEIGHBOUR 5.                                        Citizens' wives.
NEIGHBOUR 1. And knights.
NEIGHBOUR 6.                        In coaches.
NEIGHBOUR 2.                                Yes, and oyster-women.
NEIGHBOUR 1. Beside other gallants.                                  5
NEIGHBOUR 3.                        Sailors' wives.
NEIGHBOUR 4.                                        Tobacco men.
NEIGHBOUR 5. Another Pimlico!²
LOVEWIT.                        What should my knave° advance,  *servant*
To draw this company? He hung out no banners
Of a strange calf with five legs to be seen?
Or a huge lobster with six claws?
NEIGHBOUR 6.                        No, sir.

---

1   *shave ... trim*  Both verbs can also mean to trick or swindle.
2   *Pimlico*  Place of entertainment at Hoxton.

10  NEIGHBOUR 3.  We had gone in then, sir.

LOVEWIT.                                        He has no gift

Of teaching i' the nose[1] that e'er I knew of!

You saw no bills° set up that promised cure                    *posters*

Of agues, or the tooth-ache?

NEIGHBOUR 2.                          No such thing, sir.

LOVEWIT.  Nor heard a drum struck,[2] for baboons or puppets?

15  NEIGHBOUR 5.  Neither, sir.

LOVEWIT.                            What device should he bring forth now?

I love a teeming wit as I love my nourishment.

Pray God he ha' not kept such open house,

That he hath sold my hangings, and my bedding:

I left him nothing else. If he have eat 'em,

20  A plague o' the moth, say I! Sure he has got

Some bawdy pictures to call all this ging;°                        *gang*

The Friar and the Nun; or the new motion°                    *puppet show*

Of the Knight's courser covering the Parson's mare;

The boy of six year old with the great thing:

25  Or 't may be, he has the fleas that run at tilt

Upon a table, or some dog to dance?

When saw you him?

NEIGHBOUR 1.          Who, sir, Jeremy?

NEIGHBOUR 2.                            Jeremy butler?

We saw him not this month.

LOVEWIT.                          How!

NEIGHBOUR 4.                                Not these five weeks, sir.

NEIGHBOUR 1.  These six weeks, at the least.

LOVEWIT.                                        Y'amaze me, neighbours!

30  NEIGHBOUR 5.  Sure, if your worship know not where he is,

He's slipp'd away.

NEIGHBOUR 6.        Pray God, he be not made away!

LOVEWIT.  Ha? it's no time to question, then.

(*He knocks.*)

NEIGHBOUR 6.                                    About

Some three weeks since, I heard a doleful cry,

---

1   *teaching i' the nose*  Preaching like a puritan.
2   *drum struck*  To draw a crowd, for a show.

As I sat up a-mending my wife's stockings.

LOVEWIT. This 's strange! That none will answer! Didst thou hear     35
    A cry, sayst thou?

NEIGHBOUR 6.        Yes, sir, like unto a man
    That had been strangled an hour, and could not speak.

NEIGHBOUR 2. I heard it too, just this day three weeks,[1] at two o'clock
    Next morning.

LOVEWIT.       These be miracles, or you make 'em so!
    A man an hour strangled, and could not speak,     40
    And both you heard him cry?

NEIGHBOUR 3.        Yes, downward,° sir.    *definitely*

LOVEWIT. Thou art a wise fellow. Give me thy hand, I pray thee.
    What trade art thou on?

NEIGHBOUR 3.        A smith, and 't please your worship.

LOVEWIT. A smith? Then, lend me thy help to get this door open.

NEIGHBOUR 3. That I will presently, sir, but fetch my tools—     45

[*Exit.*]

NEIGHBOUR 1. Sir, best to knock again, afore you break it.


## ACT 5, SCENE 2

LOVEWIT. I will.

([*Enter*] *Face* [*who opens the door*].)

FACE.        What mean you, sir?

NEIGHBOURS 1, 2, 4.        O, here's Jeremy!

FACE. Good sir, come from the door.

LOVEWIT.        Why! What's the matter?

FACE. Yet farther, you are too near, yet.

LOVEWIT.        I' the name of wonder!
    What means the fellow?

FACE.        The house, sir, has been visited.

LOVEWIT. What? With the plague? Stand thou then farther.     5

FACE.        No, sir,

---

1  *this day three weeks*  Three weeks ago.

I had it not.

LOVEWIT.    Who had it then? I left
None else, but thee, i' the house!

FACE.                   Yes, sir. My fellow,
The cat that kept the butt'ry, had it on her
A week, before I spy'd it: but I got her
10   Convey'd away i' the night. And so I shut
The house up for a month—

LOVEWIT.            How!

FACE.                    Purposing then, sir,
T' have burnt rose-vinegar, treacle, and tar,
And ha' made it sweet, that you should ne'er ha' known it:
Because I knew the news would but afflict you, sir.

15 LOVEWIT. Breathe less, and farther off. Why, this is stranger!
The neighbours tell me all, here, that the doors
Have still been open—

FACE.         How, sir!

LOVEWIT.                Gallants, men, and women,
And of all sorts, tag-rag, been seen to flock here
In threaves,° these ten weeks, as to a second Hogsden,     *throngs*
20   In days of Pimlico and Eye-bright![1]

FACE.                   Sir,
Their wisdoms will not say so!

LOVEWIT.            Today, they speak
Of coaches, and gallants; one in a French hood
Went in, they tell me: and another was seen
In a velvet gown, at the window. Divers more
25   Pass in and out!

FACE.         They did pass through the doors then,
Or walls, I assure their eye-sights, and their spectacles;
For here, sir, are the keys, and here have been,
In this my pocket, now, above twenty days!
And for before, I kept the fort alone there.
30   But that 'tis yet not deep i' the afternoon,
I should believe my neighbours had seen double

---

1   *Eye-bright* A tavern in Hogsden.

Through the black-pot,[1] and made these apparitions!
For, on my faith to your worship, for these three weeks,
And upwards, the door has not been opened.
LOVEWIT.                              Strange!
NEIGHBOUR 1.  Good faith, I think I saw a coach.                    35
NEIGHBOUR 2.                              And I too,
  I'd ha' been sworn!
LOVEWIT.              Do you but think it now?
  And but one coach?
NEIGHBOUR 4.          We cannot tell, sir: Jeremy
  Is a very honest fellow.
FACE.                  Did you see me at all?
NEIGHBOUR 1.  No: that we are sure on.
NEIGHBOUR 2.                          I'll be sworn o' that.
LOVEWIT.  Fine rogues, to have your testimonies built on!          40


[*Enter Neighbour 3.*]


NEIGHBOUR 3.  Is Jeremy come!
NEIGHBOUR 1.                  O, yes, you may leave your tools;
  We were deceiv'd, he says.
NEIGHBOUR 2.              He has had the keys:
  And the door has been shut these three weeks.
NEIGHBOUR 3.                          Like enough.
LOVEWIT.  Peace, and get hence, you changelings.[2]
FACE.  [*Seeing Surly and Mammon about to enter.*]    Surly come!
  And Mammon made acquainted? They'll tell all.                    45
  How shall I beat them off? What shall I do?
  Nothing's more wretched, than a guilty conscience.

---

1  *Through the black-pot*  Through too much drinking. A black-pot is a beer mug.
2  *changelings*  People who change their minds; idiots. Fairies were thought to steal healthy
   babies and replace them with sick ones called changelings (cf. Thomas Middleton's play *The
   Changeling*).

# ACT 5, SCENE 3

*([Enter] Surly [and] Mammon.)*

SURLY. No, sir, he was a great physician. This,
It was no bawdy-house, but a mere chancel.[1]
You knew the lord, and his sister.

MAMMON.                                                    Nay, good Surly—

SURLY. The happy word, "be rich"—

MAMMON.                                                    Play not the tyrant—

5  SURLY. Should be today pronounced, to all your friends.
And where be your andirons now? And your brass pots?
That should ha' been golden flagons, and great wedges?

MAMMON. Let me but breathe. What! They ha' shut their doors,
Methinks!

SURLY.          Aye, now 'tis holiday with them.

*(Mammon and Surly knock.)*

MAMMON.                                                    Rogues,
10  Cozeners, impostors, bawds!

FACE.                                    What mean you, sir?

MAMMON. To enter if we can.

FACE.                                    Another man's house!
Here is the owner, sir. Turn you to him,
And speak your business.

MAMMON. *[To Lovewit.]*    Are you, sir, the owner?

LOVEWIT. Yes, sir.

MAMMON.          And are those knaves within your cheaters?

15  LOVEWIT. What knaves, what cheaters?

MAMMON.                                    Subtle and his Lungs.

FACE. The gentleman is distracted, sir! No lungs,
Nor lights[2] ha' been seen here these three weeks, sir,

---

1  *chancel*  The easternmost or holiest part of a church, used by the clergy in presenting the
   liturgy.
2  *lungs, Nor lights*  When butchers sold the lungs of animals, they called them "lights."

Within these doors, upon my word!
SURLY.                                    Your word,
   Groom arrogant!
FACE.                        Yes, sir, I am the housekeeper,
And know the keys ha' not been out o' my hands.                    20
SURLY. This 's a new Face!
FACE.                        You do mistake the house, sir!
   What sign[1] was 't at?
SURLY.                        You rascal! This is one
O' the confederacy. Come, let's get officers,
   And force the door.
LOVEWIT.                        Pray you stay,° gentlemen.                    *wait*
SURLY. No, sir, we'll come with warrant.                    25
MAMMON.                                    Aye, and then,
   We shall ha' your doors open.

   [*Exeunt Mammon and Surly.*]

LOVEWIT.                        What means this?
FACE. I cannot tell, sir!
NEIGHBOUR 1.                    These are two o' the gallants
   That we do think we saw.
FACE.                        Two o' the fools!
   You talk as idly as they. Good faith, sir,
   I think the moon has crazed 'em all.                    30

   ([*Enter*] *Kastril.*)

   [*Aside.*]                                    O me,
   The angry boy come too? He'll make a noise,
   And ne'er away till he have betrayed us all.

   (*Kastril knocks.*)

KASTRIL. What rogues, bawds, slaves, you'll open the door, anon!
   Punk, cockatrice,[2] my suster! By this light

_____

1   *What sign*   Taverns and brothels and inns all had signs; Face is trying to suggest that Surly
    and Mammon are drunkenly mistaking the house for a bar or brothel.
2   *cockatrice*   Originally a legendary monster, hatched from a cock's egg, that killed with its
    glance. Here, a prostitute.

35 I'll fetch the marshal to you. You are a whore
   To keep your castle—
FACE.                    Who would you speak with, sir?
KASTRIL. The bawdy Doctor and the cozening Captain,
   And Puss my suster.
LOVEWIT.              This is something, sure!
FACE. Upon my trust, the doors were never open, sir.
40 KASTRIL. I have heard all their tricks told me twice over,
   By the fat knight,° and the lean gentleman.°       *Mammon / Surly*
LOVEWIT. Here comes another.

   ([*Enter*] *Ananias* [*and*] *Tribulation*.)

FACE.                    Ananias too?
   And his pastor?

(*They beat too at the door.*)

TRIBULATION.    The doors are shut against us.
ANANIAS. Come forth, you seed of sulphur, sons of fire,
45 Your stench, it is broke forth: abomination
   Is in the house.
KASTRIL.         Aye, my suster's there.
ANANIAS.                        The place,
   It is become a cage of unclean birds.[1]
KASTRIL. Yes, I will fetch the Scavenger,[2] and the Constable.
TRIBULATION. You shall do well.
ANANIAS.                    We'll join, to weed them out.
50 KASTRIL. You will not come then? Punk device,°      *perfect whore*
   my suster!
ANANIAS. Call her not sister. She is a harlot, verily.
KASTRIL. I'll raise the street.
LOVEWIT.                  Good gentlemen, a word.
ANANIAS. Satan, avoid, and hinder not our zeal.

   [*Exeunt Ananias, Tribulation, and Kastril.*]

---

1   *cage of unclean birds*  Cf. Revelation, 18.2.
2   *Scavenger*  Parish officer charged with keeping the streets clean.

LOVEWIT. The world's turn'd Bet'lem.

FACE. These are all broke loose,
Out of St. Kather'ne's,[1] where they use to keep 55
The better sort of mad-folks.

NEIGHBOUR 1. All these persons
We saw go in, and out, here.

NEIGHBOUR 2. Yes, indeed, sir.

NEIGHBOUR 3. These were the parties.

FACE. Peace, you drunkards. Sir,
I wonder at it! Please you to give me leave
To touch the door, I'll try and the lock be changed. 60

LOVEWIT. It mazes me!

FACE. Good faith, sir, I believe
There's no such thing. 'Tis all *deceptio visus*–° *hallucination*
[*Aside.*] Would I could get him away.

DAPPER. [*Within.*] Master Captain, master Doctor.

LOVEWIT. Who's that?

FACE. [*Aside.*] Our clerk within, that I forgot!—I know not, sir.

DAPPER. [*Within.*] For God's sake, when will her Grace be at 65
leisure?

FACE. Ha!
Illusions, some spirit o' the air. [*Aside.*] His gag is melted,
And now he sets out the throat.[2]

DAPPER. [*Within.*] I am almost stifled—

FACE. [*Aside.*] Would you were altogether.

LOVEWIT. 'Tis i' the house.
Ha! List.

FACE. Believe it, sir, i' the air!

LOVEWIT. Peace, you—

DAPPER. [*Within.*] Mine aunt's Grace does not use me well. 70

SUBTLE. [*Within.*] You fool,
Peace, you'll mar all.

FACE. [*To Subtle within.*] Or you will else, you rogue.

LOVEWIT. O is it so? Then you converse with spirits!
Come, sir. No more o' your tricks, good Jeremy,

---

1 *St. Kather'ne's* Hospital for the mentally ill, founded in 1148 by Queen Matilda.
2 *sets out the throat* Shouts.

The truth, the shortest way.

FACE.                 Dismiss this rabble, sir.

75   [*Aside.*] What shall I do? I am catch'd.

LOVEWIT.                   Good neighbours,
I thank you all. You may depart. Come, sir,

[*Exeunt Neighbours.*]

You know that I am an indulgent master:
And therefore, conceal nothing. What's your med'cine,
To draw so many several sorts of wild-fowl?

80 FACE. Sir, you were wont to affect mirth and wit:
But here's no place to talk on 't i' the street.
Give me but leave, to make the best of my fortune,
And only pardon me th' abuse of your house:
It's all I beg. I'll help you to a widow,

85 In recompense, that you shall gi' me thanks for,
Will make you seven years younger, and a rich one.
'Tis but your putting on a Spanish cloak:
I have her within. You need not fear the house,
It was not visited.[1]

LOVEWIT.          But by me, who came

90 Sooner than you expected.

FACE.               It is true, sir.
Pray you forgive me.

LOVEWIT.         Well: let's see your widow.

[*Exeunt.*]

## ACT 5, SCENE 4

([*Enter*] Subtle [*and*] Dapper.)

SUBTLE. How! Ha' you eaten your gag?

DAPPER.               Yes faith, it crumbled
Away i' my mouth.

SUBTLE.       You ha' spoiled all then.

DAPPER.              No,

---

1  *visited*  By the plague.

I hope my aunt of Fairy will forgive me.
SUBTLE.  Your aunt's a gracious lady; but in troth
   You were to blame.                                           5
DAPPER.             The fume did overcome me,
   And I did do 't to stay my stomach. Pray you
   So satisfy° her Grace. Here comes the Captain.       *explain it to*

([*Enter*] *Face.*)

FACE.  How now? Is his mouth down?°               *gag gone*
SUBTLE.                   Aye! He has spoken!
FACE.  (A pox, I heard him, and you too.) He's undone then.
   [*Aside.*] I have been fain to say, the house is haunted     10
   With spirits, to keep churl[1] back.
SUBTLE.                   And hast thou done it?
FACE.  Sure, for this night.
SUBTLE.              Why, then triumph and sing
   Of Face so famous, the precious king
   Of present wits.
FACE.           Did you not hear the coil°         *disturbance*
   About the door?                                        15
SUBTLE.           Yes, and I dwindled with° it.     *shrank from*
FACE.  Show him his aunt, and let him be dispatched:
   I'll send her to you.

[*Exit Face.*]

SUBTLE.             Well, sir, your aunt her Grace
   Will give you audience presently,° on my suit,     *immediately*
   And the Captain's word, that you did not eat your gag,
   In any contempt of her Highness.                    20
DAPPER.               Not I, in troth, sir.

([*Enter*] *Doll like the Queen of Fairy.*)

SUBTLE.  Here she is come. Down o' your knees, and wriggle:
   She has a stately presence. Good. Yet nearer,

---

1  *churl*  The one from the country.

And bid, God save you!
DAPPER.                         Madam.
SUBTLE.                              And your aunt.
DAPPER. And my most gracious aunt, God save your Grace.
DOLL. Nephew, we thought to have been angry with you:
25   But that sweet face of yours hath turned the tide,
And made it flow with joy, that ebbed of love.
Arise, and touch our velvet gown.
SUBTLE.                              The skirts,
And kiss 'em. So.
DOLL.                    Let me now stroke that head.
*Much, nephew, shalt thou win; much shalt thou spend;*
30   *Much shalt thou give away; much shalt thou lend.*
SUBTLE. (Aye, much indeed.) Why do you not thank her Grace?
DAPPER. I cannot speak for joy.
SUBTLE.                    See, the kind° wretch!                 *natural*
Your Grace's kinsman right.
DOLL.°                         Give me the bird.°        *familiar spirit, fly*
Here is your fly in a purse, about your neck, cousin;
35   Wear it, and feed it about this day se'night,°        *week (seven-night)*
On your right wrist—
SUBTLE.                    Open a vein, with a pin,
And let it suck but once a week: till then,
You must not look on't.
DOLL.                         No. And, kinsman,
Bear yourself worthy of the blood you come on.°        *descend from*
40   SUBTLE. Her Grace would ha' you eat no more Woolsack pies,
Nor Dagger furmety.[1]
DOLL.                    Nor break his fast
In Heaven, and Hell.[2]
SUBTLE.                    She's with you everywhere!
Nor play with costermongers, at mumchance, tray-trip,
45   God-make-you-rich[3] (when as your aunt has done it), but keep

---

1 *Woolsack* A tavern in London; *Dagger* A tavern in Holborn; *furmety* Cooked wheat with milk and seasonings.
2 *Heaven and Hell* Taverns in Westminster.
3 *costermongers* Vendors selling fruit on the street; *mumchance, tray-trip* Dice games; *God-make-you-rich* A backgammon-like game.

ACT 5, SCENE 4

The gallant'st company, and the best games—
DAPPER.                                    Yes, sir.
SUBTLE.  Gleek and primero:[1] and what you get, be true to us.
DAPPER.  By this hand, I will.
SUBTLE.                      You may bring 's a thousand pound
  Before tomorrow night (if but three thousand
  Be stirring°) and you will.                         *available*  50
DAPPER.                        I swear I will then.
SUBTLE.  Your fly will learn° you all games.                *teach*
FACE.  [*Within.*]                  Ha' you done there?
SUBTLE.  Your Grace will command him no more duties?
DOLL.                                        No:
  But come, and see me often. I may chance
  To leave him three or four hundred chests of treasure,
  And some twelve thousand acres of Fairyland,            55
  If he game well and comely° with good gamesters.       *nicely*
SUBTLE.  There's a kind aunt! Kiss her departing part.
  But you must sell your forty mark a year, now.
DAPPER.  Aye, sir, I mean.
SUBTLE.                  Or, gi' 't away: pox on 't!
DAPPER.  I'll gi' 't mine aunt. I'll go and fetch the writings.  60
SUBTLE.  'Tis well, away.

[*Exit Dapper.*]

[*Enter Face.*]

FACE.                  Where's Subtle?
SUBTLE.                      Here. What news?
FACE.  Drugger is at the door, go take his suit,
  And bid him fetch a parson, presently:
  Say, he shall marry the widow. Thou shalt spend°       *earn*
  A hundred pound by the service!                       65
                  Now, Queen Doll,

[*Exit Subtle.*]

---

1  *Gleek and primero*  Cf. 2.3.284–85.

Ha' you packed up all?

DOLL.                              Yes.

FACE.                              And how do you like
The Lady Pliant?

DOLL.              A good dull innocent.°                    *simple-minded*

[*Enter Subtle.*]

SUBTLE.  Here's your Hieronimo's cloak and hat.

FACE.                                        Give me 'em.

SUBTLE.  And the ruff too?

FACE.              Yes, I'll come to you presently.

[*Exit.*]

70  SUBTLE.  Now he is gone about his project, Doll,
I told you of, for the widow.

DOLL.                        'Tis direct
Against our articles.

SUBTLE.              Well, we'll fit him, wench.
Hast thou gulled her of her jewels, or her bracelets?

DOLL.  No, but I will do 't.

SUBTLE.                    Soon at night, my Dolly,
75  When we are shipped, and all our goods aboard,
Eastward for Ratcliff, we will turn our course
To Brainford,° westward, if thou sayst the word,              *Brentford*
And take our leaves of this o'erweening rascal,
This peremptory Face.

DOLL.              Content, I'm weary of him.

80  SUBTLE.  Thou'st cause, when the slave will run a-wiving, Doll,
Against the instrument° that was drawn between us.            *agreement*

DOLL.  I'll pluck his bird as bare as I can.

SUBTLE.                              Yes, tell her,
She must by any means address some present
To th' cunning man, make him amends for wronging
85  His art with her suspicion; send a ring,
Or chain of pearl; she will be tortured else
Extremely in her sleep, say: and ha' strange things

Come to her. Wilt thou?
DOLL.                              Yes.
SUBTLE.                              My fine flitter-mouse,°              *bat*
My bird o' the night; we'll tickle it at the Pigeons,¹
When we have all, and may unlock the trunks,                    90
And say, this's mine and thine, and thine, and mine—

(*They kiss.*)

[*Enter Face.*]

FACE. What now! a-billing?²
SUBTLE.                              Yes, a little exalted
In the good passage of our stock-affairs.°          *business capital*
FACE. Drugger has brought his parson, take him in, Subtle,
And send Nab back again, to wash his Face.                    95
SUBTLE. I will: and shave himself?
FACE.                              If you can get him.

[*Exit Subtle.*]

DOLL. You are hot upon it, Face, whate'er it is!
FACE. A trick, that Doll shall spend ten pound a month by.

[*Enter Subtle.*]

Is he gone?
SUBTLE.     The chaplain waits you i' the hall, sir.
FACE. I'll go bestow him.                              100

[*Exit Face.*]

DOLL.                              He'll now marry her, instantly.
SUBTLE. He cannot yet, he is not ready. Dear Doll,
Cozen her of all thou canst. To deceive him
Is no deceit, but justice, that would break

---

1  *tickle it at the Pigeons*  Enjoy ourselves at The Three Pigeons, an inn in Brentford.
2  *a-billing*  Kissing, caressing bills, as doves do.

Such an inextricable tie as ours was.
105 DOLL. Let me alone to fit him.

[*Enter Face.*]

FACE.                         Come, my venturers,
  You ha' pack'd up all? Where be the trunks? Bring forth.
SUBTLE. Here.
FACE.           Let us see 'em. Where's the money?
SUBTLE.                                Here,
  In this.
FACE.      Mammon's ten pound; eight score before.
  The Brethren's money, this. Drugger's and Dapper's.
110 What paper's that?
DOLL.                   The jewel of the waiting maid's,
  That stole it from her lady, to know certain—
FACE. If she should have precedence of her mistress?
DOLL.                                      Yes.
FACE. What box is that?
SUBTLE.              The fish-wives' rings, I think;
  And the ale-wives' single money.° Is 't not, Doll?      *small change*
115 DOLL. Yes; and the whistle that the sailor's wife
  Brought you, to know and° her husband were with Ward.[1]      *if*
FACE. We'll wet it[2] tomorrow; and our silver-beakers,
  And tavern cups. Where be the French petticoats,
  And girdles, and hangers?[3]
SUBTLE.              Here, i' the trunk,
120 And the bolts of lawn.°                     *rolls of cloth*
FACE.              Is Drugger's damask there?
  And the tobacco?
SUBTLE.           Yes.
FACE.              Give me the keys.
DOLL. Why you the keys?
SUBTLE.              No matter, Doll: because
  We shall not open 'em before he comes.

---

1  *Ward*  Famous pirate; a pamphlet about him was published in 1609.
2  *wet it*  I.e., the whistle (pawn it for money to buy drinks).
3  *hangers*  Belt loops that hold swords.

FACE. 'Tis true, you shall not open them, indeed;
   Nor have 'em forth. Do you see? Not forth, Doll.                    125
DOLL.                                              No?
FACE. No, my smock-rampant.[1] The right is, my master
   Knows all, has pardon'd me, and he will keep 'em.
   Doctor, 'tis true (you look) for all your figures:[2]
   I sent for him, indeed. Wherefore, good partners,
   Both he and she be satisfy'd; for here                              130
   Determines° the indenture tripartite                   *concludes*
   'Twixt Subtle, Doll, and Face. All I can do
   Is to help you over the wall, o' the back-side,°   *rear of the property*
   Or lend you a sheet to save your velvet gown, Doll.
   Here will be officers presently; bethink you                       135
   Of some course suddenly to 'scape the dock:°         *prisoner's dock*
   For thither you will come else. (*Some knock.*) Hark you, thunder!
SUBTLE. You are a precious fiend!
OFFICERS. [*Within.*]                    Open the door.
FACE. Doll, I am sorry for thee, i' faith. But hear'st thou?
   It shall go hard, but I will place thee somewhere:                  140
   Thou shalt have my letter to Mistress Amo.
DOLL.                                      Hang you—
FACE. Or Madam Caesarean.[3]
DOLL.                              Pox upon you, rogue,
   Would I had but time to beat thee.
FACE.                                  Subtle,
   Let's know where you set up next; I will send you
   A customer, now and then, for old acquaintance:                    145
   What new course ha' you?
SUBTLE.                        Rogue, I'll hang myself:
   That I may walk a greater devil, than thou,
   And haunt thee i' the flock-bed and the buttery.[4]

[*Exeunt.*]

---

1  *smock-rampant*  Angry woman. In heraldry, an animal "rampant" is in an aggressive posture, on its hind legs.
2  (*you look*) Don't look at me like that;  *for all your figures* In spite of all your horoscopes
   and attempts to know the future.
3  *Mistress Amo ... Madam Caesarean*  Type-names for brothel madams.
4  *i' the flock-bed and the buttery*  Where you'll be sleeping and eating.

## ACT 5, SCENE 5

([*Enter*] *Lovewit* [*in the Spanish dress with the Parson*].)

LOVEWIT. What do you mean, my masters?
MAMMON. [*Within.*]                          Open your door,
  Cheaters, bawds, conjurers.
OFFICER. [*Without.*]        Or we will break it open.
LOVEWIT. What warrant have you?
OFFICER. [*Without.*]              Warrant enough, sir, doubt not:
  If you'll not open it.
LOVEWIT.              Is there an officer, there?
5 OFFICER. [*Without.*] Yes, two or three for° failing.        *in case of*
LOVEWIT.                                Have but patience,
  And I will open it straight.

([*Enter*] *Face* [*as Jeremy*].)

FACE.                        Sir, ha' you done?
  Is it a marriage? Perfect?
LOVEWIT.            Yes, my brain.
FACE. Off with your ruff, and cloak then. Be yourself, sir.
SURLY. [*Without.*] Down with the door.
10 KASTRIL. [*Without.*]              'Slight, ding° it open.        *smash*
LOVEWIT. [*Opening the door.*]                        Hold.
  Hold, gentlemen, what means this violence?

([*Enter*] *Mammon, Surly, Kastril, Ananias, Tribulation, Officers.*)

MAMMON. Where is this collier?
SURLY.                  And my Captain Face?
MAMMON. These day-owls.
SURLY.              That are birding[1] in men's purses.
MAMMON. Madam Suppository.°                    *imposter, whore*
KASTRIL.                Doxy,° my suster.              *whore*
ANANIAS.                              Locusts

---

1  *birding*  Catching birds (i.e., filching money).

Of the foul pit.

TRIBULATION.      Profane as Bel and the dragon.[1]

ANANIAS. Worse than the grasshoppers, or the lice of Egypt.[2]     15

LOVEWIT. Good gentlemen, hear me. Are you officers,

   And cannot stay this violence?

OFFICER.                  Keep the peace.

LOVEWIT. Gentlemen, what is the matter? Whom do you seek?

MAMMON. The chemical cozener.

SURLY.                 And the Captain pander.

KASTRIL. The nun° my suster.                     *whore*   20

MAMMON.             Madam Rabbi.[3]

ANANIAS.                       Scorpions,

   And caterpillars.

LOVEWIT.        Fewer at once, I pray you.

OFFICER. One after another, gentlemen, I charge you,

   By virtue of my staff—

ANANIAS.            They are the vessels

   Of pride, lust, and the cart.

LOVEWIT.           Good zeal, lie still

   A little while.                                 25

TRIBULATION.   Peace, Deacon Ananias.

LOVEWIT. The house is mine here, and the doors are open:

   If there be any such persons as you seek for,

   Use your authority, search on o' God's name.

   I am but newly come to town, and finding

   This tumult 'bout my door, to tell you true,             30

   It somewhat mazed me; till my man, here, fearing

   My more displeasure, told me he had done

   Somewhat an insolent part, let out my house

   (Belike, presuming on my known aversion

   From any air o' the town while there was sickness)     35

   To a Doctor and a Captain: who, what they are

---

1  *Bel and the dragon*  Apocryphal book of the Old Testament. Both images represent idol worship. Bel was a false brass image destroyed by David; the dragon was fed until it exploded.

2  *grasshoppers ... Egypt*  Plagues inflicted on Egypt to convince Pharaoh to let the Israelites go.

3  *Madam Rabbi*  Mammon is referring to Doll in her learned ravings.

Or where they be, he knows not.
MAMMON.                              Are they gone?
LOVEWIT. You may go in and search, sir.

(*They enter.*)

                                        Here, I find
The empty walls, worse than I left 'em, smoked,
40  A few cracked pots, and glasses, and a furnace,
The ceiling filled with poesies of the candle,[1]
And Madam with a dildo writ o' the walls.[2]
Only one gentlewoman, I met here,
That is within, that said she was a widow—
45 KASTRIL. Aye, that's my suster. I'll go thump her. Where is she?

[*Exit.*]

LOVEWIT. And should ha' marry'd a Spanish Count, but he,
When he came to 't, neglected her so grossly,
That I, a widower, am gone through with her.[3]
SURLY. How! Have I lost her then?
LOVEWIT.                              Were you the Don, sir?
50  Good faith, now, she docs blame you extremely, and says
You swore, and told her you had ta'en the pains
To dye your beard, and umber o'er your face,
Borrowed a suit, and ruff, all for her love;
And then did nothing. What an oversight,
55  And want of putting forward, sir, was this!
Well fare an old harquebuzier,° yet,                     *musketeer*
Could prime his powder, and give fire, and hit,
All in a twinkling.

(*Mammon comes forth.*)

MAMMON.              The whole nest are fled!
LOVEWIT. What sort of birds were they?
MAMMON.                              A kind of choughs,°   *crow-like birds*

---

1  *poesies of the candle*  Words written on the ceiling in smoke.
2  *Madam ... walls*  Lewd graffiti on the walls.
3  *am gone ... her*  Have married her (with a sexual innuendo).

Or thievish daws,° sir, that have picked my purse       *jackdaws* 60
Of eight score and ten pounds within these five weeks,
Beside my first materials; and my goods,
That lie i' the cellar, which I am glad they ha' left,
I may have home yet.
LOVEWIT.          Think you so, sir?
MAMMON.                 Aye.
LOVEWIT. By order of law, sir, but not otherwise.       65
MAMMON. Not mine own stuff?
LOVEWIT.                Sir, I can take no knowledge,
That they are yours, but by public means.
If you can bring certificate that you were gulled of 'em,
Or any formal writ, out of a court,
That you did cozen yourself: I will not hold them.       70
MAMMON. I'll rather lose 'em.
LOVEWIT.              That you shall not, sir,
By me, in troth. Upon these terms they are yours.
What should they ha' been, sir, turned into gold, all?
MAMMON.                  No,
I cannot tell. It may be they should. What then?
LOVEWIT. What a great loss in hope have you sustained!       75
MAMMON. Not I, the commonwealth has.
FACE.                 Aye, he would ha' built
The city new; and made a ditch about it
Of silver, should have run with cream from Hogsden;
That every Sunday, in Moorfields, the younkers,°    *young men*
And tits and tom-boys should have fed on, *gratis*.[1]      80
MAMMON. I will go mount a turnip-cart,° and preach    *farm cart*
The end o' the world, within these two months. Surly,
What! In a dream?
SURLY.          Must I needs cheat myself,
With that same foolish vice of honesty!
Come let us go, and hearken out° the rogues.      *search for* 85
That Face I'll mark for mine, if e'er I meet him.
FACE. If I can hear of him, sir, I'll bring you word,
Unto your lodging; for in troth, they were strangers

---

1    *tits and tom-boys*   Young girls;   *gratis*   Free.

To me, I thought 'em honest, as myself, sir.

[*Exeunt Mammon and Surly.*]

(*They* [*Ananias and Tribulation and Officers*] *come forth.*)

90  TRIBULATION.  'Tis well, the saints shall not lose all yet. Go,
    And get some carts—
    LOVEWIT.                    For what, my zealous friends?
    ANANIAS.  To bear away the portion of the righteous
    Out of this den of thieves.
    LOVEWIT.                    What is that portion?
    ANANIAS.  The goods, sometime° the orphans', that the          formerly
        brethren
95  Bought with their silver pence.
    LOVEWIT.                         What, those i' the cellar,
    The knight Sir Mammon claims?
    ANANIAS.                       I do defy
    The wicked Mammon, so do all the brethren,
    Thou profane man. I ask thee with what conscience
    Thou canst advance that idol against us,
100 That have the seal?[1] Were not the shillings numbered,
    That made the pounds? Were not the pounds told out,
    Upon the second day of the fourth week,
    In the eighth month, upon the table dormant,[2]
    The year of the last patience of the saints,[3]
105 Six hundred and ten?°                                          *1610*
    LOVEWIT.                  Mine earnest vehement botcher,°        bungler
    And Deacon also, I cannot dispute with you:
    But if you get you not away the sooner,
    I shall confute you with a cudgel.
    ANANIAS.              Sir.
    TRIBULATION.  Be patient, Ananias.
    ANANIAS.                        I am strong,
110 And will stand up, well girt, against an host

---

1  *seal*  Those who have the seal of God on their forehead are spared the torture of scor-
   pion-like stings of locusts in Revelation 9.4.
2  *table dormant*  Fixed side-table.
3  *last patience of the saints*  Last thousand years before the end of the world.

That threaten Gad in exile.[1]

LOVEWIT.                              I shall send you
To Amsterdam, to your cellar.

ANANIAS.                              I will pray there,
Against thy house: may dogs defile thy walls,
And wasps and hornets breed beneath thy roof,
This seat of falsehood, and this cave of cozenage!                    115

[*Exeunt Ananias, Tribulation, and Officers.*]

(*Drugger enters.*)

LOVEWIT.  Another too? (*And he beats him away.*)
DRUGGER.                              Not I, sir, I am no brother.
LOVEWIT. Away, you Harry Nicholas,[2] do you talk?

[*Exit Drugger.*]

FACE.  No, this was Abel Drugger.
(*To the Parson.*)                    Good sir, go,
And satisfy him; tell him, all is done:
He stayed too long a-washing of his face.                              120
The Doctor, he shall hear of him at Westchester;[3]
And of the Captain, tell him, at Yarmouth, or
Some good port-town else, lying for a wind.

[*Exit Parson.*]

If you can get off the angry child, now, sir—

([*Enter Kastril and*] *Dame Pliant.*)

---

1  *Gad in exile*  Refers to the Old Testament son of Jacob and Leah's maid Zilpah (*Genesis* 30.9–11) called Gad, whose lost portion of the territory of Israel was eventually restored.
2  *Harry Nicholas*  Sixteenth-century Anabaptist mystic and leader of a sect proscribed by Elizabeth I in 1580.
3  *Westchester*  Chester; also a tangential reference to a popular lost Elizabethan play full of trickery, *The Wise Men of Westchester*.

125 KASTRIL. Come on, you ewe, you have match'd most sweetly, ha'
    you not?
    Did not I say, I would never ha' you tupped°        *mated*
    But by a dubbed boy, to make you a lady-tom?[1]
    'Slight, you are a mammet!° O, I could touse[2] you, now.    *puppet*
    Death, mun'° you marry, with a pox!        *must*
LOVEWIT.                      You lie, boy;
130 As sound° as you; and I'm aforehand with you.    *fit*
KASTRIL.                     Anon?
LOVEWIT. Come, will you quarrel? I will feize° you, sirrah.    *beat*
    Why do you not buckle to your tools?[3]
KASTRIL.                  God's light!
    This is a fine old boy, as e'er I saw!
LOVEWIT. What, do you change your copy° now? Proceed;    *behavior*
135 Here stands my dove: stoop° at her, if you dare.    *swoop*
KASTRIL. 'Slight, I must love him! I cannot choose, i' faith!
    An I should be hanged for 't! Suster, I protest,
    I honour thee, for this match.
LOVEWIT.             O, do you so, sir?
KASTRIL. Yes, an thou canst take tobacco, and drink, old boy,
140 I'll give her five hundred pound more, to her marriage,
    Than her own state.
LOVEWIT.        Fill a pipe-full, Jeremy.
FACE. Yes; but go in and take it, sir.
LOVEWIT.            We will.
    I will be ruled by thee in anything, Jeremy.
KASTRIL. 'Slight, thou art not hide-bound! Thou art a jovy° boy!    *jovial*
145 Come, let us in, I pray thee, and take our whiffs.
LOVEWIT. Whiff in with your sister, brother boy.

[*Exeunt Kastril and Dame Pliant.*]

[*To the audience.*]
                            That master

---

1  *dubbed* Knighted; *lady-tom* If Dame Pliant marries someone knighted (or of even
    higher rank), she would be a Lady.
2  *touse* Handle roughly.
3  *buckle to your tools* Draw your weapons.

That had received such happiness by a servant,
In such a widow, and with so much wealth,
Were very ungrateful, if he would not be
A little indulgent to that servant's wit,                                    150
And help his fortune, though with some small strain
Of his own candour.° Therefore, gentlemen,                      *integrity*
And kind spectators, if I have outstript
An old man's gravity, or strict canon,° think                      *rule*
What a young wife and a good brain may do:                          155
Stretch age's truth sometimes, and crack it too.
Speak for thy self, knave.
FACE.                              So I will, sir.
    [*To the audience.*]                              Gentlemen,
My part a little fell in this last scene,
Yet 'twas decorum.¹ And though I am clean
Got off from Subtle, Surly, Mammon, Doll,                           160
Hot Ananias, Dapper, Drugger, all
With whom I traded, yet I put myself
On you, that are my country:° and this pelf°         *jury / booty*
Which I have got, if you do quit° me, rests                  *acquit*
To feast you often, and invite new guests.                          165

[*Exeunt.*]
                          THE END

---

1   *decorum*   Suitable to character.

# In Context

# On Alchemy

**from Geoffrey Chaucer, "The Canon's Yeoman's Tale," from *The Canterbury Tales*[1] (1387–1400)**

Geoffrey Chaucer's *Canterbury Tales* is a framed narrative poem containing a series of stories told by a group of pilgrims on their way from London to the shrine of Saint Thomas Becket in Canterbury. Each pilgrim is to tell a tale on the journey, and the teller of the best tale is to receive a free dinner at a London tavern when the pilgrims return.

The following is an excerpt from the tale told by a Canon's Yeoman. A yeoman is a servant, who in this case works for a clergyman (a canon), who is also an underhanded practitioner of alchemy. The yeoman mocks his master's gullible prey by explaining the alchemist's sleight of hand to his fellow pilgrims. In the tale, the canon's tricks include fooling a priest with a hollowed-out core of beechwood coal with silver filings inside, end stopped with wax. When the coal is placed in a furnace, the wax melts, and the silver is poured into the crucible, creating "alchemical silver" for the person being tricked. The alchemist then repeats the trick twice more with less valuable metals, once with mercury and once with copper. For forty pounds, he teaches the priest how to pull off the trick, netting a tidy sum. This same ruse is brought up in *The Alchemist*'s opening scene, when Face threatens to publish all of Subtle's "tricks" including "coz'ning with a hollow coal."

---

1   *The Canterbury Tales*   This excerpt is drawn from Andrew Taylor and Robert Boenig's edition of *The Canterbury Tales* for Broadview Press, 2012.

In Londoun was a preest annueleer,[1]
That therinne had dwelled many a yeer,
Which was so plesaunt° and so servysable°          *pleasant / helpful*
Unto the wyf whereas he was at table,°            *where he was lodged*
5 That she wolde suffre hym nothyng for to paye° *allow him to pay nothing*
For bord ne clothyng, wente he° never so gaye.    *he went about*
And spendyng° silver hadde°                        *spending / had*
    he right ynow.°                                *quite enough*
Therof no fors!° I wol procede as now°            *it does not matter / for now*
And telle forth my tale of the chanoun
10 That broghte this preest to confusioun.°                          *ruin*
This false chanoun cam upon a day
Unto this preestes chambre° wher he lay,                          *room*
Bisechynge° hym to lene hym a certeyn°           *asking / certain [amount]*
Of gold, and he wolde quite it hym ageyn.°           *pay it back to him*
15 "Leene° me a marc,"°[2] quod he, "but dayes three,        *lend / mark*
And at my day° I wol it quiten thee.°          *[appointed] day / give it back*
And if so be that thow me fynde fals,°                        *find me false*
Another day do hange me by the hals."°             *hang me by the neck*
This preest hym took° a marc and that as swithe,°  *gave him / quickly*
20 And this chanoun hym thanked ofte° sithe                    *many times*
And took his leve and wente forth his weye
And at the thridde day broghte his moneye,
And to the preest he took his gold agayn,
Wherof this preest was wonder glad and fayn.°                    *happy*
25 "Certes," quod he, "nothyng anoyeth me°            *it does not bother me*
To lene° a man a noble[3] or two or thre°                    *loan / three*

---

1   *annueleer*  An "annualer" priest was one who was awarded an endowment, usually from a
deceased wealthy person, to say a specific number of masses to reduce that person's time in
Purgatory. Such a priest had no care of a parish or other charitable work beyond saying these
masses. Many people considered this practice a scandal, and Chaucer praises his Parson for
not following it.

2   *marc*  A mark was worth two-thirds of a pound—for the late fourteenth century not a
negligible amount.

3   *noble*  A noble was a gold coin worth half a mark.

Or what thyng° were in my possessioun       *whatever thing*
Whan he so trewe° is of condicioun°       *true / character*
That in no wise° he breke wole his day.° *way / will miss his [appointed] day*
To swich a man I kan never seye nay."       30
"What," quod this chanoun, "sholde I be untrewe?°       *unreliable*
Nay, that were a thyng yfallen al of
     newe.°       *that would happen for the first time*
Trouthe° is a thyng that I wol evere kepe       *truth*
Into° that day in which that I shal crepe°       *until / creep*
Into my grave, or ellis God forbede!°       *forbid*   35
Bileveth° this as siker° as the Crede.°[1]       *believe / sure / Creed*
God thanke I, and in good tyme be it sayd
That ther was nevere man yet yvele apayd°       *dissatisfied*
For gold ne silver that he to me lente,
Ne nevere falshede in myn herte I mente.°       *intended*   40
And sire," quod he, "now of my pryvetee,°       *secrets*
Syn° ye so goodlich° han been unto me       *since / kind*
And kithed° to me so greet gentillesse,°       *shown / great nobility*
Somwhat to quyte° with youre kyndenesse       *pay back*
I wol yow shewe,° if that yow list to leere.°       *show you / wish to learn*   45
I wol yow teche° pleynly° the manere       *teach / plainly*
How I kan werken° in philosophie.°       *can work / alchemy*
Taketh good heede! Ye shul wel seen at eye°       *with [your] eye*
That I wol doon a maistrie° er° I go."       *marvel / before*
"Ye," quod the preest, "ye, sire," quod he, "and wol ye so?       50
Marie!° Therof° I pray yow hertely."°       *by St. Mary / for this / heartily*
"At youre comandement sire, trewely,"
Quod the chanoun, "and ellis° God forbeede!"°       *else / forbid*
Loo, how this theef koude° his service beede!°       *could / offer*
Ful sooth° it is that swich profred servyse° *very true / such offered service*   55
Stynketh,° as witnessen° thise olde wyse,°[2] *stinks / bear witness / wise ones*
And that, ful soone,° I wol it verifie.°       *soon / verify*
In this chanoun, roote° of alle trecherie,°       *root / treachery*
That evere moore delit hath and gladnesse—

---

1   *Crede* The Church required believers to learn by heart the Apostles' Creed, a basic state-
    ment of Christian belief.
2   *Stynketh ... wyse* A common proverb. Skeat notes that one version, "Proffered service
    stinketh," is found among John Heywood's *Proverbs*.

60 Swiche feendly° thoghtes in his herte impresse°—     *fiendish | crowd about*
    How Cristes peple he may to meschief brynge.°     *brings to mischief*
    God kepe° us from his false dissymulynge!°     *keep | false pretense*
    Noght wiste° this preest with whom that he delte,°     *knew | dealt*
    N'of° his harm comyng° he nothyng felte.°     *nor of | coming | felt nothing*
65 O sely preest, o sely innocent!°     *foolish*
    With coveitise° anon° thou shalt be     *coveting | immediately*
       blent!°     *blinded*
    O gracelees,° ful blynd° is thy conceite!°     *unfortunate | very blind | reason*
    Nothyng ne artow war° of the deceite     *nor are you aware*
    Which that this fox yshapen hath for thee.°     *has made for you*
70 Hise wily wrenches° thou ne mayst nat° flee.     *tricks | may not*
    Wherfore,° to go to the conclusioun     *therefore*
    That refereth to° thy confusioun,°     *pertains to | ruin*
    Unhappy° man, anon° I wol me hye°     *unlucky | immediately | hurry*
    To tellen thyn unwit and thy folye°     *your folly*
75 And eek the falsnesse of that oother wrecche
    As ferforth° as my konnyng° may strecche.°     *far | knowledge | stretch*
    This chanoun was my lord, ye wolden weene?°     *would suppose*
    Sire Hoost, in feith and by the Hevenes queene,°     *Heaven's queen (Mary)*
    It was another chanoun and nat hee
80 That kan° an hundredfoold moore subtiltee.°     *who knows | trickery*
    He hath bitrayed° folkes many tyme.     *betrayed*
    Of his falshede° it dulleth me to ryme.°     *falsehood | distresses*
    Evere whan that I speke of his falshede
    For shame of hym my chekes wexen rede,°     *cheeks grow red*
85 Algates° they bigynnen° for to glowe.°     *at least | begin | glow*
    For reednesse have I noon° right wel,° I knowe,     *none | quite well*
    In my visage,° for fumes diverse°     *face | various fumes*
    Of metals, whiche, ye han herd me reherce,°     *heard me list*
    Consumed and wasted han my reednesse.°     *red complexion*
90 Now taak heede of this chanons cursednesse.
    "Sire," quod he to the preest, "lat youre man gon
    For quyksilver,° that° we hadde° it anon,°     *mercury | so that | have | at once*
    And lat hym bryngen ounces two or three.

And whan he comth, as faste shal ye see
A wonder thyng which ye saugh° nevere er° this."          *saw / before*     95
"Sire," quod the preest, "it shal be doon, ywis!"°                    *indeed*
He bad° his servant fecchen° hym this thyng,          *commanded / to fetch*
And he al redy was at his biddyng,
And wente hym forth and cam anon agayn°                 *came back at once*
With this quyksilver, soothly° for to sayn,°               *truly / say*    100
And took thise ounces thre to the chanoun.
And he hem leyde faire and wel adoun°          *put them carefully down*
And bad the servant coles° for to brynge,                            *coals*
That he anon myghte go to his werkynge.°                       *experiment*
The coles right anon weren yfet,°                            *were fetched*    105
And this chanoun took out a crosselet°                            *crucible*
Of his bosom° and shewed° it to the preest.          *chest / showed*
"This instrument," quod he, "which that thou seest,
Taak in thyn hand, and put thyself therinne°               *put it in yourself*
Of this quyksilver an ounce, and heer bigynne°               *here begin*    110
In name of Crist, to wexe a philosofre.°          *become an alchemist*
Ther been ful fewe to whiche I wolde profre°                        *offer*
To shewen hem thus muche of my science.°                      *knowledge*
For ye shul seen heer° by experience                                *here*
That this quyksilver wol I mortifye[1]                                        115
Right in youre sighte anon°—I wol nat lye°—          *immediately / will not lie*
And make as good silver and as fyn°                                  *fine*
As ther is any in youre purs° or myn°                        *purse / mine*
Or elleswhere, and make it
     malliable,°          *malleable (capable of being worked with a hammer)*
And elles° holdeth me fals and unable                           *otherwise*    120
Amonges folk forevere to appeere.°                                *appear*
I have a poudre° heer° that coste° me deere,°     *powder / here / cost / dearly*
Shal° make al good, for it is cause of al                       *[That] shall*
My konnyng,° which that I to yow shewen shal.                  *knowledge*
Voyde° youre man, and lat hym° be          *send away / let him*    125
     theroute,°                                                       *outside*

---

1   *quyksilver ... mortifye*   To mortify or kill quick (i.e., live) silver (or what we now call mer-
    cury) is to solidify or transform it into silver. Unlike modern chemistry, medieval learning,
    which placed a great deal of importance on etymology, held that quick silver and normal
    silver were related at some fundamental level.

And shette° the dore° whils we been aboute     *shut / door*
Oure pryvetee,° that no man us espie°     *secrets / spy*
Whils that we werke in this philosophie."°     *discipline (alchemy)*
Al as he bad° fulfilled° was in dede.°     *commanded / done / deed*
130 This ilke° servant anonright° out yede,°     *same / right away / went*
And his maister shette the dore anon,
And to hire labour spedily they gon.
This preest, at this cursed chanons biddyng,
Upon the fir anon sette this thyng°     *thing (the crucible)*
135 And blew the fir and bisyed hym° ful faste.     *busied himself*
And this chanoun into the crosselet caste
A poudre. Noot° I wherof° that it was     *do not know / of what*
Ymaad,° outher° of chalk or of glas°     *made / either / glass*
Or somwhat elles,° was nat° worth a flye,°     *something else / not / fly*
140 To blynde° with the preest, and bad     *blind*
    hym hye°     *ordered him to hurry*
The coles for to couchen° al above     *arrange*
The crosselet. "For in tokenyng° I thee love,"     *token*
Quod this chanoun, "thyne owene handes two
Shul werche al thyng which shal heer be do."°     *shall do everything*
145 "Grauntmercy,"° quod the preest and was ful glad     *thank you*
And couched° cole as that chanoun bad.°     *arranged / commanded*
And whil he bisy was, this feendly wrecche,°     *fiendish wretch*
This false chanoun—the foule feend hym fecche°—     *seize him*
Out of his bosom he took a bechen cole°     *piece of beechwood charcoal*
150 In which ful subtilly° was maad° an hole,     *cleverly / made*
And therinne put was of silver lemaille°     *silver filings*
An ounce, and stopped was withouten faille,°     *without fail*
This hole with wex,° to kepe the lemaille in.     *wax*
And understondeth that this false gyn°     *mechanism*
155 Was nat maad ther, but it was maad bifore,
And othere thynges° I shal tellen moore°     *other things / more*
Herafterward,° whiche that he with hym broghte     *afterwards*
Er he cam there, hym to bigile,° he thoghte.     *trick*
And so he dide, er that they wente atwynne.°     *separated*
160 Til he had terved hym,° he koude nat     *cheated him*
    blynne.°     *could not stop*
It dulleth° me whan that I of hym speke.     *depresses*

On his falshede fayn wolde° I me wreke,°     *would gladly / avenge*
If I wiste° how, but he is heere and there.     *knew*
He is so variaunt,° that he abit° nowhere.     *changeable / stays*
But taketh heede° now, sires, for Goddes love!     *take heed*   165
He took this cole of which I spak above,
And in his hand he baar it pryvely,°     *carried it secretly*
And whils the preest couched bisily°     *busily arranged*
The coles, as I tolde yow er this,
This chanoun seyde, "Freend, ye doon amys.°     *do wrong*   170
This is nat couched as it oghte be.
But soone I shal amenden it,"° quod he.     *shall make it better*
"Now lat me medle therwith° but a while,     *meddle with it*
For of yow have I pitee, by Seint Gile.[1]
Ye been right hoot.° I se wel how ye swete.°     *hot / sweat*   175
Have heere a clooth and wipe awey the wete."
And whils that the preest wiped his face,
This chanoun took his cole with harde
      grace°     *with bad luck i.e., curse him*
And leyde° it above upon the myddeward°     *placed / middle part*
Of the crosselet and blew wel afterward     180
Til that the coles gonne faste brenne.°     *began to burn fast*
"Now yeve° us drynke," quod the chanoun thenne.     *give*
"As swithe° al shal be wel, I undertake.°     *quickly / declare*
Sitte we doun, and lat us myrie make."°     *make merry*
And whan that this chanouns bechen cole     185
Was brent,° al the lemaille° out of the hole     *burned / metal filings*
Into the crosselet fil anon adoun.
And so it moste nedes° by resoun,°     *must necessarily / reason*
Syn° it so evene aboven it couched° was.     *since / arranged*
But therof° wiste° the preest nothyng, allas!     *of it / knew*   190
He demed° alle the coles yliche° good,     *thought / equally*
For of that sleighte,° he nothyng understood.     *trick*
And whan this alkamystre° saugh° his tyme,° *alchemist / saw / opportunity*
"Ris° up," quod he, "sire preest, and sit by me.     *rise*
And for° I woot wel° ingot have I noon,°     *since / know well / none*   195

---

1   *Seint Gile* St. Giles was a seventh-century hermit from Provence, in what is now southern
    France. In popular belief, an invocation to him allows a sinner to omit confessing his sins
    out loud to a priest.

Gooth, walketh forth,° and bryng us a chalk stoon.°    *walk out / stone*
For I wol make oon of the same shape
That is an ingot, if I may han hape.°                    *have luck*
And bryngeth eek° with yow a bolle° or a panne°        *also / bowl / pan*
200 Ful of water, and ye shul se wel thanne°            *see well then*
How that oure bisynesse° shal thryve° and            *business / shall thrive*
    preeve.°                                            *succeed*
And yet, for° ye shul han no mysbileeve°              *so that / doubt*
Ne wrong conceite° of me in youre absence,           *idea*
I ne wol nat been° out of youre presence,            *will not be*
205 But go with yow and come with yow ageyn."
The chambre dore, shortly for to seyn,
They opened and shette and wente hir weye.°          *their way*
And forth with hem they carieden° the keye°          *carried / key*
And coome agayn withouten any delay.
210 What sholde I tarien° al the longe day?           *delay*
He took the chalk and shoope° it in the wise°        *shaped / way*
Of an ingot, as I shal yow devyse.°                   *describe*
I seye he took out of his owene sleeve
A teyne° of silver—Yvele moot he cheeve!°—           *rod / bad luck to him*
215 Which that was nat but an ounce of weighte.
And taak heede° now of his cursed sleighte.°         *take heed / trick*
He shoope his ingot in lengthe and eek in breede°    *breadth*
Of this teyne,° withouten any drede,°                *rod / fear*
So slyly, that the preest it nat espide.°            *did not see it*
220 And in his sleve agayn he gan it hide.°           *hid it*
And fro the fir he took up his mateere,°             *material*
And in th'yngot putte° it with myrie cheere.°        *put / merry expression*
And in the water vessel he it caste°                 *threw*
Whan that hym luste° and                              *he wished*
    bad° the preest as faste,                         *commanded*
225 "What that heer is, put in thyn hand and grope.
Thow fynde shalt° ther° silver, as I hope."          *shall find / there*
[What—devel of Helle!—schold it elles be?
Shavyng of silver silver is, parde!]¹

---

1  Ellesmere omits these two lines, but they are found in numerous later manuscripts. They are
   supplied here from Harley 7334.

He putte his hand in and took up a teyne° — *rod*
Of silver fyn, and glad in every veyne° — *vein* — 230
Was this preest. Whan he saugh it was so,
"Goddes blessyng and his moodres also
And alle halwes° have ye,° sire chanoun," — *saints / you*
Seyde this preest. "And I hir malisoun,° — *curse her*
But and° ye vouchesauf° to techen° me — *unless / promise / teach* — 235
This noble craft and this subtiltee,° — *cleverness*
I wol be youre in al that evere I may!"° — *in all things as best as I can*
Quod the chanoun,[1] "Yet wol I make assay° — *will I try*
The seconde tyme, that ye may taken heede° — *take heed*
And been expert of this. And in youre neede — 240
Another day, assaye° in myn absence — *try*
This disciplyne and this crafty science.° — *clever knowledge*
Lat take another ounce," quod he tho,
"Of quyksilver withouten wordes mo
And do therwith as ye han doon° er° this — *have done / before* — 245
With that oother, which that now silver is."
This preest hym bisieth° in al that he kan° — *busies himself / can*
To doon as this chanoun, this cursed man,
Comanded hym. And faste he blew the fir
For to come to th'effect° of his desir. — *the attainment* — 250
And this chanoun, right in the meenewhile,° — *meanwhile*
Al redy was the preest eft° to bigile.° — *again / trick*
And, for a contenaunce,° in his hand he bar° — *the appearance / carried*
An holwe stikke°—taak kepe° and bewar— — *hollow stick / take heed*
In the ende of which an ounce and namoore — 255
Of silver lemaille° put was, as bifore, — *filings*
In his cole and stopped with wex weel,° — *well with wax*
For to kepe in his lemaille every deel.° — *every part*
And whil this preest was in his bisynesse,° — *was busy*
This chanoun with his stikke gan hym dresse° — *went* — 260
To hym anon and his poudre° caste in — *powder*
As he dide er. The devel° out of his skyn° — *devil / skin*
Hym terve,° I pray to God, for his falshede!° — *flay him / falsehood*
For he was evere fals in thoght and dede.

---

1   *chanoun*  Ellesmere reads "preest" here. The emendation is from Harley 7334.

265 And with this stikke above the crosselet°          *crucible*
      That was ordeyned° with that false jet,°          *prepared | device*
      He stired the coles til relente gan°              *began to soften*
      The wex° agayn the fir,° as every man,            *wax | with the fire*
      But° it a fool be, woot wel° it moot              *unless | knows well*
         nede,°                                          *must necessarily*
270 And al that in the stikke was out yede,°            *gone out*
      And in the crosselet hastily it fel.°            *fell*
      Now, good sires, what wol ye bet than wel?[1]
      Whan that this preest thus was bigiled° ageyn,   *tricked*
      Supposynge° noght but treuthe, sooth to seyn,    *supposing*
275 He was so glad, that I ne kan nat expresse
      In no manere his myrthe and his gladnesse.
      And to the chanoun he profred eftsoone°          *offered at once*
      Body and good.° "Ye," quod the chanoun soone,°   *possessions | at once*
      "Though povre° I be, crafty° thou shalt           *poor | skillful*
         me fynde.°                                      *shall find me*
280 I warne thee, yet is ther moore bihynde.°          *more to come*
      Is ther any coper° herinne?" seyde he.            *copper*
      "Ye," quod the preest, "sire, I trowe wel° ther be." *believe well*
      "Elles go bye° us som,° and that as swithe.°     *buy | some | quickly*
      Now, good sire, go forth thy wey and hythe."°    *hurry*
285 He wente his wey and with the coper cam,
      And this chanoun it in hise handes nam°          *took*
      And of that coper weyed° out but° an ounce.      *weighed | only*
      Al to symple° is my tonge to pronounce,°         *too simple | express*
      As ministre° of my wit, the doublenesse°         *minister | deceit*
290 Of this chanoun, roote of alle cursednesse!
      He semed freendly to hem that knewe hym noght,°  *did not know him*
      But he was feendly° bothe in herte and thoght.   *fiendish*
      It weerieth° me to telle of his falsnesse,       *wearies*
      But nathelees yet wol I it expresse
295 To th'entente° that men may bewar therby°          *the intent | beware of it*
      And for noon oother cause, trewely.°             *truly*
      He putte the ounce of coper in the crosselet,

---

1  *what ... wel*  "What do you wish better than well?"; in other words, "what could be better?"

And on the fir as swithe° he hath it set,                              *quickly*
And caste in poudre and made the preest to blowe
And in his werkyng for to stoupe lowe°                          *stoop low*   300
As he dide er. And al nas° but a jape!°                     *was not / joke*
Right as hym liste,° the preest he made his          *just as he wished*
    ape.°                                                                        *monkey*
And afterward in the ingot he it caste°                              *threw*
And in the panne° putte it at the laste.°              *pan / at last*
Of the water in he putte his owene hand,                                        305
And in his sleve,° as ye bifornhand°                   *sleeve / beforehand*
Herde me telle, hadde a silver teyne.°                                *rod*
He slyly took it out, this cursed heyne,°                       *scoundrel*
Unwityng this preest of his false craft,[1]
And in the pannes botme he hath it laft°              *has left it*   310
And in the water rombled[2] to and fro
And wonder pryvely° took up also                    *very secretly*
The coper teyne, noght knowynge this preest,°   *without the priest knowing*
And hidde it and hym hente° by the breest°        *grabbed him / breast*
And to hym spak and thus seyde in his game:°              *trick*   315
"Stoupeth adoun,° by God! Ye be to blame.°   *stoop down / you are to blame*
Helpeth me now, as I dide yow whil eer.°         *I earlier did to you*
Putte in youre hand, and looketh what is theer."
This preest took up this silver teyne anon,
And thanne seyde the chanoun, "Lat° us gon,°          *let / go*   320
With thise thre teynes whiche that we han wroght,°      *made*
To som goldsmyth and wite° if they been                    *find out*
    oght.°                                                     *are [worth] anything*
For, by my feith, I nolde for myn hood,
But if that they were silver fyn and good.[3]
And that as swithe preeved° it shal bee."             *quickly proven*   325
Unto the goldsmyth with thise teynes three
They wente and putte thise teynes in assay°                  *in trial*
To fir and hamer. Myghte no man seye nay,°      *no one could say no*
But that they weren as hem oghte be.°            *as they ought to be*

---

1  *Unwityng … craft*  "The priest not knowing of his treacherous skill."
2  *rombled*  The word is rare. *The Middle English Dictionary* suggests it means "to cause a
   rumbling sound by movement" (s.v., *rumbelen*, e).
3  *For … good*  "For, by my faith, I would not wish them to be anything but silver and gold."

| | |
|---|---|
| 330   This sotted° preest, who was gladder than he? | *foolish* |
| Was nevere brid° gladder agayn the day° | *bird / for the dawn* |
| Ne nyghtyngale in the sesoun of May. | |
| Nas nevere man that luste bet to synge,° | *wished to sing better* |
| Ne lady lustier° in carolynge° | *more pleasantly / singing* |
| 335   Or for to speke of love and wommanhede,° | *womanhood* |
| Ne knyght in armes to doon an hardy dede° | *do any courageous deed* |
| To stonden° in grace° of his lady deere | *stand / favor* |
| Than hadde this preest this soory craft° to leere.° | *sorry skill / learn* |
| And to the chanoun thus he spak and seyde, | |
| 340   "For love of God that for us alle deyde,° | *died* |
| And as I may deserve it unto yow, | |
| What shal this receite° coste, telleth° now?" | *recipe / tell [me]* |
| "By oure Lady," quod this chanoun, "it is deere.° | *expensive* |
| I warne yow wel, for,° save I and a frere,° | *except / friar* |
| 345   In Engelond° ther kan no man it make." | *MS Egelond* |
| "No fors,"° quod he. "Now sire, for Goddes sake, | *it matters not* |
| What shal I pay? Telleth me, I preye." | |
| "Ywis,"° quod he, "it is ful deere, I seye. | *indeed* |
| Sire, at o° word, if that thee list it have,° | *one / if you wish to have it* |
| 350   Ye shul paye fourty pound,¹ so God me save. | |
| And nere° the freendshipe that ye dide er this | *were not* |
| To me, ye sholde paye moore, ywis."° | *indeed* |
| This preest the somme of fourty pound anon | |
| Of nobles° fette° and took hem everichon | *gold coins / fetched* |
| 355   To this chanoun for this ilke° receit.° | *same / recipe* |
| Al his werkyng° nas° but fraude and deceit. | *working / was not* |
| "Sire Preest," he seyde, "I kepe° han no loos° | *desire / praise* |
| Of° my craft, for I wolde it kept were cloos.° | *from / kept secret* |
| And as ye love me, kepeth it secree,° | *keep it secret* |
| 360   For and° men knewen° al my soutiltee,° | *if / knew / cleverness* |
| By God, they wolden han so greet envye° | *great envy* |
| To me bycause of my philosophye,° | *learning* |
| I sholde be deed. Ther were noon oother weye!"° | *no other way* |
| "God it forbeede," quod the preest. "What sey ye? | |

---

1   *fourty pound*   Forty pounds was a considerable sum; in fact it was the official annual amount that qualified one to become a knight and thus was the lower end of an income considered wealthy.

| | | |
|---|---|---|
| Yet hadde I levere spenden° al the good° | *rather spend / possessions* | 365 |
| Which that I have or elles wexe I wood,° | *become crazy* | |
| Than that ye sholden falle in swich mescheef."° | *into such misfortune* | |
| "For youre good wyl, sire, have ye right good preef,"° | *proof* | |
| Quod the chanoun. "And farwel! Grantmercy!"° | *thank you* | |
| He went his wey, and never the preest hym sy° | *saw him* | 370 |
| After that day. And whan that this preest shoolde° | *should* | |
| Maken assay° at swich tyme° as he wolde | *attempt / such a time* | |
| Of this receit, farwel, it wolde nat be.° | *would not be* | |
| Lo thus byjaped° and bigiled° was he. | *tricked / beguiled* | |
| Thus maketh he his introduccioun° | *he (the canon) prepares the way* | 375 |
| To brynge folk to destruccioun. | | |

## Desiderius Erasmus, "The Alchemist"[1] (1524)

Desiderius Erasmus was a Dutch philosopher who has long been recognized as one of the most important writers of the Early Modern
period. "The Alchemist" is one of the dialogues included in his book
the *Colloquies*, which he began writing in the 1490s as exercises in
Latin for his students. Erasmus published these first in 1518 and grad-
ually began to add longer dialogues. The final edition, published in
1533, included fifty dialogues, all of them guiding readers with mild
humor toward the humanist values that Erasmus argued for throughout his life. The dialogues cover a wide array of subjects, from alchemy
to pilgrimages, from motherhood and breastfeeding to marriage and
friendship. The *Colloquies* were widely read and remained influential
across Europe throughout the early modern period.

THE ARGUMENT.
This colloquy[2] shows the dotage of an old man, otherwise a very pru-
dent person, upon this art;[3] being tricked by a priest, under pretence
of a two-fold method in this art, the long way and the short way.
By the long way he puts an egregious cheat upon old Balbinus: the
alchemist lays the fault upon his coals and glasses. Presents of gold are

---

1   *The Alchemist*   "The Alchymist," from *The Colloquies of Erasmus*, volume 1, translated by
    Nathan Bailey and edited by Rev. E. Johnson, 1878.
2   *colloquy*   Dialogue.
3   *this art*   I.e., alchemy.

sent to the Virgin Mary, that she would assist them in their undertakings. Some courtiers having come to the knowledge that Balbinus
practised this unlawful art, are bribed. At last the alchemist is dis-
charged, having money given him to bear his charges.

([*Enter*] *Philecous, Lalus.*)

PHILECOUS.   What news is here, that Lalus laughs to himself so
    that he even giggles again, every now and then signing himself
    with the sign of the Cross? I'll interrupt his felicity. God bless
    you heartily, my very good friend Lalus; you seem to me to be
    very happy.
LALUS.   But I shall be much happier, if I make you a partaker of
    my merry conceitedness.[1]
PHILECOUS.   Prithee, then, make me happy as soon as you can.
LALUS.   Do you know Balbinus?
PHILECOUS.   What, that learned old gentleman that has such a very
    good character in the world?
LALUS.   It is as you say; but no man is wise at all times, or is with-
    out his blind side. This man, among his many good qualifica-
    tions, has some foibles: he has been a long time bewitched with
    the art called *alchemy*.
PHILECOUS.   Believe me, that you call only foible, is a dangerous
    disease.
LALUS.   However that is, notwithstanding he had been so often
    bitten by this sort of people, yet he has lately suffered himself to
    be imposed upon again.
PHILECOUS.   In what manner?
LALUS.   A certain priest went to him, saluted him with great
    respect, and accosted him in this manner: most learned Bal-
    binus, perhaps you will wonder that I, being a stranger to you,
    should thus interrupt you, who, I know, are always earnestly
    engaged in the most sacred studies. Balbinus gave him a nod, as
    was his custom; for he is wonderfully sparing of his words.
PHILECOUS.   That's an argument of prudence.

---

1   *conceitedness*  Wit.

LALUS.    But the other, as the wiser of the two, proceeds. You will
forgive this my importunity, when you shall know the cause of
my coming to you. Tell me then, says Balbinus, but in as few
words as you can. I will, says he, as briefly as I am able. You
know, most learned of men, that the fates of mortals are various;
and I can't tell among which I should class myself, whether
among the happy or the miserable; for when I contemplate my
fate on one part, I account myself most happy, but if on the
other part, I am one of the most miserable. Balbinus pressing
him to contract his speech into a narrow compass; I will have
done immediately, most learned Balbinus, says he, and it will
be the more easy for me to do it, to a man who understands the
whole affair so well, that no man understands it better.
PHILECOUS.    You are rather drawing an orator than an alchemist.
LALUS.    You shall hear the alchemist by and by. This happiness,
   says he, I have had from a child,[1] to have learned that most
   desirable art, I mean alchemy, the very marrow of universal
   philosophy. At the very mention of the name alchemy, Balbinus
   raised himself a little, that is to say, in gesture only, and fetch-
   ing a deep sigh, bid him go forward. Then he proceeds: but
   miserable man that I am, said he, by not falling into the right
   way! Balbinus asking him what ways those were he spoke of;
   good sir, says he, you know (for what is there, most learned sir,
   that you are ignorant of?) that there are two ways in this Art,
   one which is *called the longation, and the other which is called
   the curtation.* But by my bad Fate, I have fallen upon *longation.*
   Balbinus asking him, what was the difference of the ways; it
   would be impudent in me, says he, to mention this to a man,
   to whom all things are so well known, that nobody knows
   them better; therefore I humbly address myself to you, that you
   would take pity on me, and vouchsafe to communicate to me
   that most happy way of *curtation.* And by how much the better
   you understand this art, by so much the less labour you will
   be able to impart it to me: do not conceal so great a gift from
   your poor brother that is ready to die with grief. And as you
   assist me in this, so may Jesus Christ ever enrich you with more

---

1  *from a child*  From childhood.

sublime endowments. He thus making no end of his solemnity of obtestations,[1] Balbinus was obliged to confess, that he was entirely ignorant of what he meant by *longation* and *curtation*, and bids him explain the meaning of those words. Then he began; although sir, says he, I know I speak to a person that is better skilled than myself, yet since you command me I will do it: those that have spent their whole life in this divine art, change the species of things two ways, the one is shorter, but more hazardous, the other is longer, but safer. I account myself very unhappy, that I have laboured in that way that does not suit my genius, nor could I yet find out any body who would show me the other way that I am so passionately desirous of; but at last God has put it into my mind to apply myself to you, a man of as much piety as learning; your learning qualifies you to answer my request with ease, and your piety will dispose you to help a Christian brother, whose life is in your hands. To make the matter short, when this crafty fellow, with such expressions as these, had cleared himself from all suspicion of a design, and had gained credit, that he understood one way perfectly well, Balbinus's mind began to have an itch to be meddling. And at last, when he could hold no longer, away with your methods, says he, of *curtation*, the name of which I never heard before, I am so far from understanding it. Tell me sincerely, do you thoroughly understand longation? Phoo! says he, perfectly well; but I don't love the tediousness of it. Then Balbinus asked him, how much time it would take up. Too much, says he; almost a whole year; but in the mean time it is the safest way. Never trouble yourself about that, says Balbinus, although it should take up two years, if you can but depend upon your art. To shorten the story: they came to an agreement, that the business should be set on foot privately in Balbinus's house, upon this condition, that he should find art, and Balbinus money; and the profit should be divided between them, although the imposter modestly offered that Balbinus should have the whole gain. They both took an oath of secrecy, after the manner of those that are initiated into mysterious secrets; and presently

---

1 *obtestations* Requests, entreaties.

money is paid down for the artist to buy pots, glasses, coals, and other necessaries for furnishing the laboratory: this money our alchemist lavishes away on whores, gaming, and drinking.

PHILECOUS.   This is one way, however, of changing the species of things.

LALUS.   Balbinus pressing him to fall upon the business; he replies, don't you very well know, that *what's well begun is half done?* It is a great matter to have the materials well prepared. At last he begins to set up the furnace; and here there was occasion for more gold, as a bait to catch more: for as a fish is not caught without a bait, so alchemists must cast gold in, before they can fetch gold out. In the meantime, Balbinus was busy in his accounts; for he reckoned thus, if one ounce made fifteen, what would be the product of two thousand; for that was the sum that he determined to spend. When the alchemist had spent this money and two months' time, pretending to be wonderfully busy about the bellows and the coals, Balbinus enquired of him, whether the business went forward? At first he made no answer; but at last he urging the question, he made him answer, as all great works do; the greatest difficulty of which is, in entering upon them: he pretended he had made a mistake in buying the coals, for he had bought oaken ones, when they should have been beechen or fir ones. There was a hundred crowns gone; and he did not spare to go to gaming again briskly. Upon giving him new cash, he gets new coals, and then the business is begun again with more resolution than before; just as soldiers do, when they have happened to meet with a disaster, they repair it by bravery. When the laboratory had been kept hot for some months, and the golden fruit[1] was expected, and there was not a grain of gold in the vessel (for the chemist had spent all that too) another pretence was found out, that the glasses they used, were not rightly tempered: for, *as every block will not make a mercury,*[2] so gold will not be made in any kind of glass. And by

---

1   *golden fruit*   I.e., the gold made by the Philosopher's Stone, which was said to turn base metals to gold.
2   *every block ... mercury*   The source of this saying is unknown, but it likely refers to the rarity of mercury deposits, or to the difficulty of deriving mercury alchemically.

how much more money had been spent, by so much the loather
he was to give it over.

PHILECOUS.    Just as it is with gamesters,[1] as if it were not better to
lose some than all.

LALUS.    Very true. The chemist swore he was never so cheated since
he was born before; but now having found out his mistake, he
could proceed with all the security in the world, and fetch up
that loss with great interest. The glasses being changed, the laboratory is furnished the third time: then the operator told him,
the operation would go on more successfully, if he sent a present
of crowns[2] to the Virgin Mary, that you know is worshipped at
Paris; for it was an holy act: and in order to have it carried on
successfully, it needed the favour of the saints. Balbinus liked
this advice wonderfully well, being a very pious man, that never
let a day pass, but he performed some act of devotion or other.
The operator undertakes the religious pilgrimage; but spends
this devoted money in a bawdy-house in the next town: then
he goes back, and tells Balbinus that he had great hope that all
would succeed according to their mind, the Virgin Mary seemed
so to favour their endeavours. When he had laboured a long
time, and not one crumb of gold appearing, Balbinus reasoning
the matter with him, he answered, that nothing like this had
ever happened all his days to him, though he had so many times
had experience of his method; nor could he so much as imagine
what should be the reason of this failing. After they had beat
their brains a long time about the matter, Balbinus bethought
himself, whether he had any day missed going to chapel, or
saying the horary prayers,[3] for nothing would succeed, if these
were omitted. Says the imposter, you have hit it. Wretch that
I am, I have been guilty of that once or twice by forgetfulness,
and lately rising from table, after a long dinner, I had forgot to
say the salutation of the Virgin. Why then, says Balbinus, it is
no wonder, that a thing of this moment succeeds no better. The
trickster undertakes to perform twelve services for two that he
had omitted, and to repay ten salutations for that one. When

---

1  *gamesters*  Gamblers.
2  *crowns*  Coins worth about five shillings each.
3  *horary prayers*  Daily prayers at set times of day.

money every now and then failed this extravagant operator, and he could not find out any pretence to ask for more, he at last bethought himself of this project. He comes home like one frighted out of his wits, and in a very mournful tone cries out, O Balbinus I am utterly undone, undone; I am in danger of my life. Balbinus was astonished, and was impatient to know what was the matter. The Court, says he, have gotten an inkling of what we have been about, and I expect nothing else but to be carried to gaol immediately. Balbinus, at the hearing of this, turned pale as ashes; for you know it is capital with us,[1] for any man to practice alchemy without a license from the Prince. He goes on: not, says he, that I am afraid of death myself, I wish that were the worst that would happen, I fear something more cruel. Balbinus asking him what that was, he replied, I shall be carried away into some castle, and there be forced to work all my days, for those I have no mind to serve. Is there any death so bad as such a life? The matter was then debated, Balbinus being a man that very well understood the art of rhetoric, casts his thoughts every way, if this mischief could be prevented any way. Can't you deny the crime, says he? By no means, says the other; the matter is known among the courtiers, and they have such proof of it that it can't be evaded, and there is no defending of the fact; for the law is point-blank against it. Many things having been proposed, but coming to no conclusion, that seemed feasible; says the alchemist, who wanted present money, O Balbinus we apply ourselves to slow counsels, when the matter requires a present remedy. It will not be long before they will be here that will apprehend me, and carry me away into tribulation. And last of all, seeing Balbinus at a stand, says the alchemist, I am as much at a loss as you, nor do I see any way left, but to die like a man, unless you shall approve what I am going to propose, which is more profitable than honourable; but necessity is a hard chapter. You know these sort of men are hungry after money, and so may be the more easily bribed to secrecy. Although it is a hard case to give these rascals money to throw away; but yet, as the case now stands, I see no better

---

1 *capital with us* Punishable by death in our country.

way. Balbinus was of the same opinion, and he lays down thirty guineas[1] to bribe them to hush up the matter.

PHILECOUS. Balbinus was wonderful liberal,[2] as you tell the story.

LALUS. Nay, in an honest cause, you would sooner have gotten his teeth out of his head than money. Well, then the alchemist was provided for, who was in no danger, but that of wanting money for his wench.

PHILECOUS. I admire Balbinus could not smoke[3] the roguery all this while.

LALUS. This is the only thing that he's soft in, he's as sharp as a needle in any thing else. Now the furnace is set to work again with new money; but first, a short prayer is made to the Virgin Mary to prosper their undertakings. By this time there had been a whole year spent, first one obstacle being pretended, and then another, so that all the expense and labour was lost. In the mean time there fell out one most ridiculous chance.

PHILECOUS. What was that?

LALUS. The alchemist had a criminal correspondence with a certain courtier's lady: The husband beginning to be jealous, watched him narrowly, and in the conclusion, having intelligence that the priest was in the bed-chamber, he comes home before he was looked for, knocks at the door.

PHILECOUS. What did he design to do to him?

LALUS. What! Why nothing very good, either kill him or geld him. When the husband being very pressing to come, threatened he would break open the door, if his wife did not open it, they were in bodily fear within, and cast about for some present resolution; and circumstances admitting no better, he pulled off his coat, and threw himself out of a narrow window, but not without both danger and mischief, and so got away. Such stories as these you know are soon spread, and it came to Balbinus's ear, and the chemist guessed it would be so.

PHILECOUS. There was no getting off of this business.

LALUS. Yes, he got off better here, than he did out at the window. Hear the man's invention: Balbinus said not a word to him

---

1 *guineas* Gold coins.
2 *liberal* Generous.
3 *smoke* I.e., smoke out, detect.

about the matter, but it might be read in his countenance, that he was no stranger to the talk of the town. The chemist knew Balbinus to be a man of piety, and in some points, I was going to say, superstitious, and such persons are very ready to forgive one that falls under his crime, let it be never so great; therefore, he on purpose begins a talk about the success of their business, complaining, that it had not succeeded as it used to do, and as he would have it; and he wondered greatly, what should be the reason of it: upon this discourse, Balbinus, who seemed otherwise to have been bent upon silence, taking an occasion, was a little moved: it is no hard matter, says he, to guess what the obstacle is. Sins are the obstacles that hinder our success, for pure works should be done by pure persons. At this word, the projector[1] fell down on his knees, and beating his breast with a very mournful tone, and dejected countenance, says, O Balbinus, what you have said is very true, it is sin, it is sin that has been the hinderance; but my sins, not yours; for I am not ashamed to confess my uncleanness before you, as I would before my most holy Father Confessor: the frailty of my flesh overcame me, and Satan drew me into his snares; and O miserable wretch that I am! Of a priest, I am become an adulterer; and yet, the offering that you sent to the Virgin Mother, is not wholly lost neither, for I had perished inevitably, if she had not helped me; for the husband broke open the door upon me, and the window was too little for me to get out at; and in this pinch of danger, I bethought myself of the blessed Virgin, and I fell upon my knees, and besought her, that if the gift was acceptable to her, she would assist me, and in a minute I went to the window (for necessity forced me so to do) and found it large enough for me to get out at.

PHILECOUS.   Well, and did Balbinus believe all this?

LALUS.   Believe it, yes, and pardoned him too, and admonished him very religiously, not to be ungrateful to the blessed Virgin. Nay, there was more money laid down, upon his giving his promise, that he would for the future carry on the process with purity.

---

1   *projector*   I.e., alchemist.

PHILECOUS.   Well, what was the end of all this?

LALUS.   The story is very long; but I'll cut it short. When he had played upon Balbinus long enough with these inventions, and wheedled him out of a considerable sum of money, a certain gentleman happened to come there, that had known the knave from a child. He easily imagining that he was acting the same part with Balbinus, that he had been acting everywhere, admonishes Balbinus privately, and acquainted him what sort of a fellow he harboured, advising him to get rid of him as soon as possible, unless he had a mind to have him sometime or other to rifle[1] his coffers, and then run away.

PHILECOUS.   Well, what did Balbinus do then? Sure, he took care to have him sent to gaol?

LALUS.   To gaol? Nay, he gave him money to bear his charges, and conjured him by all that was sacred, not to speak a word of what had happened between them. And in my opinion, it was his wisdom so to do, rather than to be the common laughing-stock, and table-talk, and run the risk of the confiscation of his goods besides; for the imposter was in no danger; he knew no more of the matter than an ass, and cheating is a small fault in these sort of cattle. If he had charged him with theft, his ordination would have saved him from the gallows, and nobody would have been at the charge of maintaining such a fellow in prison.

PHILECOUS.   I should pity Balbinus; but that he took pleasure in being gulled.

LALUS.   I must now make haste to the hall; at another time I'll tell you stories more ridiculous than this.

PHILECOUS.   When you shall be at leisure, I shall be glad to hear them, and I'll give you story for story.

---

1   *rifle*   Steal from, plunder.

**from Martin Ruland, *A Lexicon of Alchemy*[1] (1612)**

The following are some examples of definitions from the alchemical dictionary by Martin Ruland (1569–1611), an alchemist employed by Holy Roman Emperor Rudolf II. Ruland's other works include *The True Method for Completing the Philosopher's Stone* (1606) and *Defense of Alchemy* (1607).

AMALGAMA    is a composition of gold or silver and quicksilver. ...

[SOL] AURUM    Gold, called sol by chemists, and dedicated to the sun, is the most tempered of all the metals; it is said to be warm and dry in the second grade, and red in the third grade. It is a metallic body, of citrine colour, effulgent, heavy, equably digested in the womb of earth, washed with mineral water during a very long time. It is composed of pure living silver, fixed, and of a clear red; also of a clean, fixed, red, incombustible sulphur. In fine, it is the most subtle substance[2] of quicksilver. Truly we have beheld quicksilver absorbing gold which it receives most willingly, even as a mother receives her son. Further, gold consists of a small quantity of clean sulphur and of a pure redness; the greater the quantity of vivific silver, the more does it derive from the mother than from the father. Purest sulphur copulating as father with quicksilver as mother, generates finest gold as a son. Briefly, coagulate quicksilver, together with sulphur, like a pure fire, yet not burning, produces gold. This is that beloved son which nature ever intends to beget, after which she ever strives; but various accidents intervene and procreate the other metals. Now gold is duplex-native[3] and prepared by fire. ...

DISTILLATIO    Distilling, Humid Elevation, is that process by which the more subtle humid parts, elevated into an ethereal consistence, and collecting on the cold roof of the alembic,[4] are condensed into moisture and pass off in drops through a pipe, to be received in another vessel. It is performed after this manner. The matter to be distilled is put into a cucurbit[5] of sufficient amplitude and not of

---

1    *A Lexicon of Alchemy*    Translated from the Latin by John Watkins, 1893.
2    *substance*    Element or part.
3    *duplex-native*    Born of two, in this case mercury and sulfur.
4    *alembic*    Vessel used for distillation.
5    *cucurbit*    Gourd-shaped vessel used for distillation.

less height (for the height occupies the artificers in vessels and the amplitude controls the height); thereupon is placed a great alembic, which easily receives the ascending spirit and resolves it into moisture. Afterwards, on account of the matter that is to be elevated, a fire is prepared, which shall be adequate to the business and contiguous to the receptacle of the moisture which is to be treated. The latter, however, is to be well shielded at all points from the flame, which must be graduated until all the humidity has passed through the alembic. We may take an instance from vegetable substances. I fill a cucurbit a third part full of fresh roses and place it in a cold water bath. Afterwards, I fill an alembic with the leaves of red roses, from which the useless thorns have been removed, and place it over the cucurbit; then I make a fire of the branches contiguous to the receptacle and to the juncture of the vessels. The moisture ascending occupies the alembic; the tincture is extracted from the roses, and, condensed into water, distils rose-red into the receptacle. It is to be noted that, if the thorns are not removed, it is impossible for the water to have the pure rose-red tint. I keep up the continuous heat until no further moisture rises up, and the roses in the alembic have become white. I have cited this because of the artifice whereby the tincture is extracted from roses by their own moisture. This method of elevation is very much in use. For we avail ourselves thereof when we extract or elaborate anything by means of the bladder, as also when we elevate a substance by means of an alembic joined to a cucurbit. ...

DRACO   is Mercury, also the Black Raven, or the Black on the Floor. It devours the tail, drinks the mercury. It is called Salt and Sulphur of the Dragons. It is the earth from the body of the sun. It is killed when it loses the soul, and rises again when the soul returns. The Dragon devours the mercury, like a poison, and dies; again drinks it and is made living. If he puts off all impurities he becomes white and truly living. This is also called the woman who kills her husband, and is herself killed in return. ...

ELEVATIO   Elevation, is Rarefaction, when the spiritual portions of a substance are elevated from the corporeal portions, the subtle raised from the gross, the volatile from the fixed, in the form of a vapour, by the power of fire, and are condensed at the top of the vessel. It is either dry or humid. ...

LAC VIRGINIS   is Mercurial Water, the Dragon's Tail; it washes and coagulates without any manual labour; it is the mercury of the philosophers, Lunar and Solar Sap, out of catholic[1] earth and water. ...

LAPIS PHILOSOPHICUS[2]   is the most potent virtue[3] concentrated by art in the centre. Outwardly, it is a tincture. Or it is that universal medicine by which age is renewed in youth, metals are transmuted, and all diseases cured. It was made by Theophrastus.[4] It is the Stone of the Wise whereby the imperfect metals are improved. ...

LUNA   i.e., silver. Sometimes a Month of Four Weeks. ...

MENSTRUUM   is that from which all metals are derived. It is of two kinds. One is like unto whey, and this is useless. The other is mercurial, and this is of good account. It is the mercury wherein gold is dissolved. The whey is the superfluous moisture which comes from the matrix and cannot be dried. Consequently, when the solution is obtained it appears in the form of a menstruous blood. Our water is a fire, a salt; fire, the true universal Menstruum of Vegetables, stronger than the fire of wood, since it transmutes the physical gold into a spirit, the Fontin Vinum Aminaeum,[5] Vinegar, the Water of the King of the Philosophers, the Genuine Extracting Solvent and Universal Vegetative Menstruum, without which the Sun and the Moon cannot be prepared, neither black nor white. ...

MERCURIUS   Mercury is the material principle, gaseous, of a watery nature, subject to generation; by its virtue shape is formed or impressed upon all things, and all things receive their perfection.

MERCURY   is mentioned everywhere, in every alchemical work, and is supposed to perform everything. Everybody wastes his brain and his money in endeavouring to produce a quantity of it. Now, mercury is a thick gluey liquid, yet it does not stick, for it is of a dry nature, moist and warm water, almost inseparably mixed with earth, so that they either remain together, or depart together.

---

1   *catholic*   Universal.
2   *Lapis Philosophicus*   Latin: philosopher's stone.
3   *virtue*   Strength, magical power.
4   *Theophrastus*   Likely refers to Theophrastus Paracelsus (c. 1493–1541), a Swiss physician, alchemist, and astrologer.
5   *Fontin Vinum Aminaeum*   Latin: Fountain of Aminaean wine.

# On Criminals and "Coney-Catching"

Popular from the mid-sixteenth to early seventeenth centuries, "rogue literature" is a genre of sensational pamphlets that vividly describe the kinds of criminals and criminal schemes that readers might expect to encounter in London and in provincial towns. Many of these pamphlets also provided glossaries so that people could interpret the slang said to be used by thieves and prostitutes; one such term was "coney-catching," tricking victims out of their money. While the extent to which rogue literature accurately described the English urban underworld is unclear, these pamphlets influenced the portrayal of thieves, prostitutes, and other criminals in many works of early modern fiction.

*The Alchemist*'s rogues and tricksters are slicker and more professional than many of those described in rogue literature, but Face, Subtle, and Doll are certainly drawn from the same tradition. The following dialogue from Robert Greene's popular pamphlet *A Disputation Between a He Cony-Catcher and a She Cony-Catcher* highlights the prowess of the "female rogue," prefiguring the character of Doll in *The Alchemist*.

**from Robert Greene, *A Disputation Between a He Cony-Catcher and a She Cony-Catcher, Whether a Thief or a Whore Is Most Hurtful in Cozenage to the Commonwealth. Discovering the secret villainies of alluring strumpets, With the conversion of an English courtesan, reformed this present year, 1592. Read, laugh and learn. Nascimur pro patria. R.G.[1] (1592)***

A disputation between Laurence, a foist, and Fair Nan, a traffic,[2] whether a whore or a thief is most prejudicial.[3]

---

1    *Nascimur pro patria*   Latin: We are born for the homeland. Many pamphlets in this genre stated patriotic aims, for example to help rid the land of criminality;   *R.G.*   Robert Greene (1558–92), English playwright. The text reprinted here was prepared through consultation with early print editions and G.B. Harrison's edition of *The thirde & last part of conny-catching* (1923); spelling and punctuation have been modernized for this volume.
2    *foist* Pick-pocket;   *traffic* Prostitute.
3    *prejudicial* Damaging (to the commonwealth).

LAURENCE.   Fair Nan, well met. What news about your Vine
Court[1] that you look so blithe? Your cherry cheeks discovers
your good fare, and your brave apparel betrays a fat purse. Is
fortune now of late grown so favourable to foists, that your
husband hath lighted on some large purchase,[2] or hath your
smooth looks linked in some young novice to sweat for a favour
all the bite in his bung,[3] and to leave himself as many crowns as
thou hast good conditions, and then he shall be one of Pierce
Peniless's[4] fraternities? How is it, sweet wench—Goes the world
on wheels, that you tread so daintily on your tiptoes?

NAN.   Why, Laurence, are you pleasant or peevish, that you quip
with such brief girds?[5] Think you a quarter-wind[6] cannot make
a quick sail, that easy lists[7] cannot make heavy burdens, that
women have not wiles to compass crowns[8] as well as men? Yes
and more, for though they be not so strong in the fists, they be
more ripe in their wits, and 'tis by wit that I live and will live, in
despite of that peevish scholar that thought with his cony-catching books to have crossbit[9] our trade. Dost thou marvel to see
me thus brisked?[10] Fair wenches cannot want favours while the
world is so full of amorous fools. Where can such girls as myself
be blemished with a threadbare coat as long as country farmers
have full purses, and wanton citizens pockets full of pence?

LAURENCE.   Truth if fortune so favour thy husband that he be
neither smoked nor cloyed,[11] for I am sure all thy bravery comes
by his nipping, foisting and lifting.[12]

---

1   *Vine Court*   A tavern, where Nan might "hold court."
2   *purchase*   Plunder.
3   *bite in his bung*   Money in his purse.
4   *Pierce Peniless*   Title character of Thomas Nashe's popular pamphlet *Pierce Penniless, His
Supplication to the Divell* (1592).
5   *quip ... girds*   Attempt wit in such fits and starts.
6   *quarter-wind*   Wind blowing on a ship's quarter.
7   *lists*   Appetites, pleasures.
8   *compass crowns*   Contrive to steal money (crowns were silver coins worth five shillings).
9   *peevish scholar ... cony-catching books*   Reference to Greene and his rogue literature
pamphlets; *crossbit* Attacked.
10   *brisked*   Animated; well-dressed.
11   *smoked nor cloyed*   Found out or burdened (perhaps by being placed in the stocks).
12   *bravery*   Fine clothes and cheerfulness; *nipping* Purse-cutting; *foisting* Pick-pock-
eting; *lifting* Stealing.

NAN.  In faith, sir, no. Did I get no more by mine own wit, than
I reap by his purchase, I might both go bare and penniless the
whole year, but mine eyes are stales, and my hands lime-twigs,[1]
else were I not worthy the name of a she cony-catcher. Circe
had never more charms, Calypso more enchantments, the
Sirens[2] more subtle tunes than I have crafty sleights to inveigle
a Cony and fetch in a country farmer. Laurence, believe me,
you men are but fools: your gettings is uncertain, and yet you
still fish for the gallows. Though by some great chance you light
upon a good bung,[3] yet you fast a great while after, whereas,
as we mad wenches have our tenants (for so I call every simple
lecher and amorous fox) as well out of term as in term to bring
us our rents.[4] Alas, were not my wits and my wanton pranks
more profitable than my husband's foisting, we might often go
to bed supperless for want of surfeiting, and yet I dare swear, my
husband gets a hundred pounds a year by bungs.

LAURENCE.  Why Nan, are you grown so stiff,[5] to think your
fair looks can get as much as our nimble fingers, or that your
sacking[6] can gain as much as our foisting? No, no, Nan, you are
two bows[7] down the wind, our foist will get more than twenty
the proudest wenches in all London.

NAN.  Lie a little further and give me some room. What Laurence
your tongue is too lavish, all stands upon proof, and since I have
leisure and you no great business, as being now when Paul's[8] is
shut up and all purchasies[9] and conies in their burrows, let us to
the tavern and take a room to ourselves, and there for the price

---

1  *stales*  Decoy-birds, used to lure other birds into a net;  *lime-twigs*  Branches covered
   with lime, a sticky substance, to trap birds.

2  *Circe … Calypso … Sirens*  Female figures in Greek mythology who ensnare men into
   doing what they want.

3  *bung*  Purse.

4  *tenants … rents*  Nan uses the metaphor of a landlord and tenant to describe the financial
   gains of prostitution. The "terms" referred to are the periods of the year when judicial
   business was done, bringing lawyers, clerks, and plaintiffs into the city.

5  *stiff*  Proud.

6  *sacking*  Bedding.

7  *two bows*  I.e., the length of two bows.

8  *Paul's*  St. Paul's Cathedral in London. In the late sixteenth and seventeenth centuries,
   petty criminals tended to gather in this cathedral and the busy public area surrounding it.

9  *purchasies*  Likely means "purchasers," i.e., buyers, customers.

of our suppers I will prove that women, I mean of our faculty, a traffic, or as base knaves term us, strumpets, are more subtle, more dangerous in the commonwealth, and more full of wiles to get crowns, than the cunningest foist, nip, lift, pragges,[1] or whatsoever that lives at this day.

LAURENCE.   Content, but who shall be moderator in our contro-versies, since in disputing pro and contra[2] betwixt ourselves, it is but your yea and my nay, and so neither of us will yield to other's victories.

NAN.   Trust me Laurence, I am so assured of the conquest, offering so in the strength of mine own arguments, that when I have reasoned, I will refer it to your judgment and censure.

LAURENCE.   And trust me as I am an honest man, I will be indifferent.[3]

NAN.   Oh swear not so deeply, but let me first hear what you can say for yourself.

LAURENCE.   What? Why more, Nan, than can be painted out in a great volume, but briefly this. I need not describe the laws of villainy because R.G. hath so amply penned them down in *The First Part of Cony-catching*,[4] that though I be one of the faculty, yet I cannot discover[5] more than he hath laid open. Therefore first to the gentleman foist. I pray you, what finer quality, what art is more excellent, either to try the ripeness of the wit, or the agility of the hand than that for him that will be master of his trade must pass the proudest juggler alive, the points of legerde-main.[6] He must have an eye to spy the bung or purse, and then a heart to dare to attempt it, for this by the way, he that fears the Gallows shall never be [a] good thief while he lives. He must as the cat watch for a mouse, and walk Paul's, Westminster, the

---

1   *pragges* Tricksters.
2   *pro and contra* Latin: for and against.
3   *indifferent* Impartial.
4   *R.G. ... Cony-catching* Refers to Robert Greene's pamphlet *A Notable Discovery of Cosen-age, Now Daily Practised by Sundry Lewd Persons, called Conie-catchers, and Cross-biters* (1591).
5   *discover* Reveal.
6   *legerdemain* Clever use of the hands when carrying out conjuring tricks.

Exchange,[1] and such common-haunted places, and there have a
curious eye to the person, whether he be a gentleman, citizen or
farmer, and note either where his bung lies, whether in his hose
or pockets, and then dog the party into a press where his stale[2]
with heaving and shoving shall so molest him, that he shall not
feel when we strip him of his bung although it be never so fast
or cunningly couched about him. What poor farmer almost can
come to plead his case at the bar, to attend upon his lawyers
at the bench, but look he never so narrowly to it, we have his
purse, wherein sometime there is fat purchase, twenty or thirty
pounds, and I pray you, how long would one of your traffics be,
earning so much with your chamber work? Besides, in fairs and
markets, and in the circuits after judges,[3] what infinite money
is gotten from honest-meaning men, that either busy about
their necessary affairs, or carelessly looking to their crowns,
light[4] amongst us that be foists? Tush, we dissemble in show,
we go so neat in apparel, so orderly in outward appearance,
some like lawyers' clerks, others like serving-men that attended
there about their masters' business, that we are hardly smoked,
versing upon all men with kind courtesies and fair words, and
yet being so warily watchful that a good purse cannot be put up
in a fair but we sigh if we share it not amongst us. And though
the books of cony-catching hath somewhat hindered us, and
brought many brave foists to the halter,[5] yet some of our country farmers, nay, of our gentleman and citizens, are so careless in
a throng of people that they show us the prey, and so draw on
a thief, and bequeath us their purses whether we will or no. For
who loves wine so ill, that he will not eat grapes if they fall into
his mouth, and who is so base that if he see a pocket fair before
him, will not foist in if he may, or if foisting will not serve, use
his knife and nip, for although there be some foists that will

---

1  *Westminster, the Exchange*  Two more busy places in London where pick-pockets would
   find victims.
2  *stale*  Decoy.
3  *circuits after judges*  I.e., following judges who are "making the circuit," traveling through
   designated areas to hold court sessions.
4  *light*  Find themselves.
5  *halter*  Gallows.

not use their knives, yet I hold him not a perfect workman or master of his mystery[1] that will not cut a purse as well as foist a pocket, and hazard any limb for so sweet a gain as gold. How answer you me this brief objection, Nan? Can you compare with either our cunning to get our gains in purchase?

NAN.    And have you no stronger arguments, Goodman Laurence, to argue your excellency in villainy but this? Then in faith put up your pipes, and give me leave to speak. Your chop-logic hath no great subtlety, for simpl[y] you reason of foisting, and appropriate that to yourselves, to you men I mean, as though there were not women foists and nips as neat in that trade as you, of as good an eye, as fine and nimble a hand, and of as resolute a heart. Yes, Laurence, and your good mistresses in that mystery, for we without like suspicion can pass in your walks under the colour of simplicity to Westminster, with a paper in our hand as if we were distressed women that had some supplication to put up to the judges, or some bill of information to deliver to our lawyers, when, God knows, we shuffle in for a bung as well as the best of you all, yea, as yourself, Laurence, though you be called King of Cutpurses, for though they smoke you, they will hardly mistrust us. And suppose our stomach stand against it to foist, yet who can better play the stale or the shadow[2] than we, for in a thrust or throng if we shove hard, who is he that will not favour a woman, and in giving place to us, give you free passage for his purse? Again, in the market, when every wife hath almost her hand on her bung, and that they cry "Beware the cutpurse and cony-catchers," then I as fast as the best, with my handbasket as mannerly as if I were to buy great store of butter and eggs for provision of my house, do exclaim against them with my hand on my purse, and say the world is bad when a woman cannot walk safely to market for fear of these villainous cutpurses, when as the first bung I come to, I either nip or foist, or else stale another while he hath stroken,[3] dispatched, and gone. Now, I pray you, gentle sir, wherein are we inferior to you in foisting? And yet this is nothing to the

---

1   *mystery*  Art.
2   *shadow*  Accomplice.
3   *stale ... stroken*  Acted as decoy for another while he has struck.

purpose, for it is one of our most simplest shifts.[1] But yet I pray you, what think you when a farmer, gentleman or citizen come to the term, perhaps he is wary of his purse, and watch him never so warily yet he will never be brought to the blow, is it not possible for us to pinch him ere he pass? He that is most chary of his crowns abroad, and will cry: "Ware the cony-catchers," will not be afraid to drink a pint of wine with a pretty wench, and perhaps go to a trugging-house[2] to ferry out one for his purpose. Then with what cunning we can feed the simple fop, with what fair words, sweet kisses, feigned sighs, as if at that instant we fell in love with him that we never saw before. If we meet him in an evening in the street, if the farmer or other whatsoever be not so forward as to motion some courtesy to us, we straight insinuate into his company, and claim acquaintance of him by some means or other, and if his mind be set for lust, and the devil drive him on to match himself with some dishonest wanton, then let him look to his purse, for if he do but kiss me in the street I'll have his purse for a farewell, although he never commit any other act at all. I speak not this only by myself Laurence, for there be a hundred in London more cunning than myself in this kind of cunny-catching.[3]

But if he come into a house then let our trade alone to verse upon him,[4] for first we feign ourselves hungry for the benefit of the house, although our bellies were never so full, and no doubt the good pander or bawd, she comes forth like a sober matron and sets store of cates[5] on the table, and then I fall aboard on them, and though I can eat little, yet I make havoc of all, and let him be sure every dish is well sauced, for he shall pay for a pipping pie[6] that cost in the market four pence, at one of the trugging-houses eighteen pence. Tush, what is dainty if it be not

---

1   *shifts*   Schemes.
2   *trugging-house*   Brothel.
3   *cunny-catching*   Alternative spelling for coney-catching; "cunny" also refers to female genitalia.
4   *verse upon him*   Defraud him.
5   *cates*   Food; purchased delicacies.
6   *pipping pie*   I.e., pippin pie, a sweet apple pie.

dear[1] bought? And yet he must come off for crowns[2] besides, and when I see him draw to his purse, I note the putting up of it well, and ere we part, that world goes hard if I foist him not of all that he hath. And then suppose the worst, that he miss it,[3] am I so simply acquainted or badly provided that I have not a friend, which with a few terrible oaths, and countenance set as if he were the proudest soldado that ever bare arms against Don John of Austria,[4] will face him quite out of his money and make him walk like a woodcock homeward by Weeping Cross,[5] and so buy repentance with all the crowns in his purse? How say you to this Laurence, whether are women foists inferior to you in ordinary cozenage or no? ...

---

1   *dear*   Expensively.

2   *come off for crowns*   Reach for or hand over money.

3   *miss it*   Notices the purse is gone.

4   *soldado*   Spanish: soldier;   *Don John of Austria*   Respected admiral and military commander, Don John of Austria (1547–78) was the illegitimate son of Holy Roman Emperor Charles V and half-brother to King Philip II of Spain.

5   *homeward by Weeping Cross*   Proverbial phrase suggesting that a person has endured a serious disappointment.

**from Thomas Harman, *A Caveat or Warning for Common Cursetors vulgarely called Vagabonds* (1566; revised 1567/68)**

Harman's *Caveat* is an early and influential example of rogue literature. In this woodcut, rogue Nicholas Blunt is depicted in two costumes, on the left as what Harman describes as an "Upright Man," a beggar who pretended to be a gentleman or soldier in distressed circumstances; on the right, Blunt—using the name Jennings—is wearing the costume of the "Counterfeit Crank," a beggar who would earn sympathy by pretending to have "falling sickness"—epilepsy.

Frequent costume changes are crucial for the success of the various criminal schemes in *The Alchemist*, as the characters shift into different roles in their plots to fool their various gulls.

The text beneath the image reads as follows:

> These two pictures lively set out,
> One body and soul, God send him more grace:
> This monstrous dissembler, a crank all about.
> Uncomely coveting of each to embrace,
> Money or wares, as he made his race.
> And sometime a mariner, and a serving man:
> Or else an artificer, as he would feign then.
> Such shifts he used, being well tried,
> Abandoning labour till he was espied.
> Conding[1] punishment for his dissimulation,
> He surely received with much declination.[2]

---

1  *Conding*  Deserving (from "condign").
2  *declination*  Reluctance.

A vpright man     The coulterfet
Nicolas    Blunt      Nicolas      Cranke
                        Genynges

    These two pyctures, lyuely set out,
One bodye and soule, god send him more grace:
    This mounstrous dessembelar, a Cranke allabout.
Vncomly coueting e, of eche to imbrace,
Money or wares, as he made his race,
And sometyme a marynar, and a saruinge man:
    Or els an artificer, as he would fayne than.
Such shyftes he vsed, beinge well tryed,
    A bandoninge labour, tyll he was espyed.
Conding punishment, for his dissimulation,
    He sewerly receaued with much declination.

# On Playwriting

## from Aristotle, *Poetics*[1]

In remarking on the design of Jonson's plots, critics often discuss the playwright's adherence to the Aristotelian unities. In Aristotle's musings about dramatic art in his *Poetics*, he famously commits to the idea of a single coherent causal narrative with a rational, clear-sighted interconnection of parts, in which the action of the play takes place within a day (unity of time), is "complete" (unity of action), and unfolds in one location (unity of place). Jonson generally follows Aristotle's advice. In this decision Jonson diverges from Shakespeare, whose plays generally do not follow the unities.

In the portion of the *Poetics* that has come down to us, Aristotle is more concerned with tragedy than comedy, but the following excerpts are suggestive of the kind of drama Jonson admired.

### 4.1–3
Poetry in general seems to have spring from two causes, each of them lying deep in our nature. First, the instinct of imitation is implanted in man from childhood, one difference between him and other animals being that he is the most imitative of living creatures; and through imitation he learns his earliest lessons; and no less universal is the pleasure felt in things imitated.

### 4.6
Imitation, then, is one instinct of our nature. Next, there is the instinct for "harmony" and rhythm, metres being manifestly sections of rhythm. Persons, therefore, starting with this natural gift developed by degrees their special aptitudes, till their rude improvisations gave birth to poetry.

---

1 *Poetics* The following excerpts are drawn from S.H. Butcher's 1902 edition of his translation of the *Poetics*.

5.1

Comedy is, as we have said, an imitation of a lower type—not, however, in the full sense of the word bad, the ludicrous being merely a subdivision of the ugly. It consists in some defect or ugliness which is not painful or destructive. It is a sort of mistake, an ugliness that does not give pain or cause destruction. To take an obvious example, the comic mask is ugly and distorted, but does not imply pain.

6.14

The plot, then, is the first principle, and, as it were, the soul of a tragedy: character holds second place.

6.17

Character is that which reveals moral purpose, showing what kind of things a man chooses or avoids. Speeches, therefore, which do not make this manifest, or in which the speaker does not choose or avoid anything whatever, are not expressive of character.

7.2–3

Now, according to our definition, Tragedy is an imitation of an action that is complete, and whole, and of a certain magnitude[.] ... A whole is that which has a beginning, a middle, and an end. A beginning is that which does not itself follow anything by causal necessity, but after which something naturally is or comes to be. An end, on the contrary, is that which itself naturally follows some other thing, either by necessity, or as a rule, but has nothing following it. A middle is that which follows something as some other thing follows it. A well constructed plot, therefore, must neither begin nor end at haphazard, but conform to these principles.

8.4

As therefore, in the other imitative arts, the imitation is one when the object imitated is one, so the plot, being an imitation of an action, must imitate one action and that a whole, the structural union of the parts being such that, if any one of them is displaced or removed, the whole will be disjointed and disturbed. For a thing whose presence or absence makes no visible difference, is not an organic part of the whole.

9.3–4

Poetry ... is a more philosophical and a higher thing than history: for poetry tends to express the universal, history the particular. By the universal I mean how a person of a certain type will on occasion speak or act, according to the law of probability or necessity; and it is this universality at which poetry aims in the names she attaches to the personages.

9.9

It clearly follows that the poet or "maker" should be the maker of plots rather than of verses; since he is a poet because he imitates, and what he imitates are actions.

15.6

As in the structure of the plot, so too in the portraiture of character, the poet should always aim either at the necessary or the probable. Thus a person of a given character should speak or act in a given way, by the rule either of necessity or of probability; just as this event should follow that by necessary or probable sequence.

**from Ben Jonson, *Timber, or Discoveries made upon men and matter as they have flowed out of his daily Readings, or had their reflux to his peculiar Notion of the Times* (1641)**

> *Timber, or Discoveries* is a commonplace book—a scrapbook of thoughts and reflections—that Jonson wrote in the course of his reading. The following excerpts reveal some of his opinions about moral life, and also some thoughts about the art of playwrighting.

A Fame that is wounded to the world would be better cured by another's apology than its own: for few can apply medicines well themselves. Besides, the man that is once hated, both his good and his evil deeds oppress him. He is not easily emergent. ...

Natures that are hardened to evil you shall sooner break than make straight; they are like poles that are crooked and dry, there is no attempting them. ...

Many men believe not themselves what they would persuade others; and less do the things which they would impose on others; but least of all know what they themselves most confidently boast. Only they set the sign of the cross over their outer doors, and sacrifice to their gut and their groin in their inner closets. ...

Puritanus Hypocrita est Hæreticus, quem opinio propriæ perspicaciæ, quâ sibi videtur, cum paucis in Ecclesiâ dogmatibus errores quosdam animadvertisse, de statu mentis deturbavit: unde sacro furore percitus, phrenetice pugnat contra magistratus, sic ratus obedientiam præstare Deo.[1] ...

Money never made any man rich, but his mind. He that can order himself to the law of Nature is not only without the sense but the fear of poverty. O! but to strike blind the people with our wealth and pomp is the thing! What a wretchedness is this, to thrust all our riches outward, and be beggars within; to contemplate nothing but the little, vile, and sordid things of the world; not the great, noble, and precious! We serve our avarice, and, not content with the good of the earth that is offered us, we search and dig for the evil that is hidden. God offered us those things, and placed them at hand, and near us, that He knew were profitable for us, but the hurtful He laid deep and hid. Yet do we seek only the things whereby we may perish, and bring them forth, when God and Nature hath buried them. We covet superfluous things, when it were more honour for us if we would contemn necessary. What need hath Nature of silver dishes, multitudes of waiters, delicate pages, perfumed napkins? She requires meat only, and hunger is not ambitious. Can we think no wealth enough but such a state for which a man may be brought into a premunire,[2] begged, proscribed, or poisoned? O! if a man could restrain the fury of his gullet and groin, and think how many fires, how many kitchens, cooks, pastures, and ploughed lands; what orchards, stews,

---

1  *Puritanus ... Deo*  Latin: A Puritan is a heretical hypocrite, in whom the conviction of his own cleverness, by which he seems to himself to have observed a few errors in Church dogmas, has disturbed the balance of his mind, so that, excited by a sacred fury, he fights frenetically against the authorities, believing that by doing so he shows obedience to God.
2  *premunire*  Predicament.

ponds and parks, coops and garners,[1] he could spare; what velvets, tissues, embroideries, laces, he could lack; and then how short and uncertain his life is; he were in a better way to happiness than to live the emperor of these delights, and be the dictator of fashions; but we make ourselves slaves to our pleasures, and we serve fame and ambition, which is an equal slavery. Have not I seen the pomp of a whole kingdom, and what a foreign king could bring hither? Also to make himself gazed and wondered at—laid forth, as it were, to the show—and vanish all away in a day? And shall that which could not fill the expectation of few hours, entertain and take up our whole lives, when even it appeared as superfluous to the possessors as to me that was a spectator? The bravery was shown, it was not possessed; while it boasted itself it perished. It is vile, and a poor thing to place our happiness on these desires. Say we wanted them all. Famine ends famine. …

*Of the magnitude and compass of any fable, epic or dramatic. What the measure of a fable is. The fable or plot of a poem defined. The epic fable, differing from the dramatic.*
To the resolving of this question we must first agree in the definition of the fable. The fable is called the imitation of one entire and perfect action, whose parts are so joined and knit together, as nothing in the structure can be changed, or taken away, without impairing or troubling the whole, of which there is a proportionable magnitude in the members. As for example: if a man would build a house, he would first appoint a place to build it in, which he would define within certain bounds; so in the constitution of a poem, the action is aimed at by the poet, which answers place in a building, and that action hath his largeness, compass, and proportion. But as a court or king's palace requires other dimensions than a private house, so the epic asks a magnitude from other poems, since what is place in the one is action in the other; the difference is [i]n space. So that by this definition we conclude the fable to be the imitation of one perfect and entire action, as one perfect and entire place is required to a building. By perfect, we understand that to which nothing is wanting, as place to the building that is raised, and action to the fable that is formed.

---

1   *garners*  Buildings where grain is stored.

It is perfect, perhaps not for a court or king's palace, which requires a greater ground, but for the structure he would raise; so the space of the action may not prove large enough for the epic fable, yet be perfect for the dramatic, and whole. ...

*What we understand by whole.*

Whole we call that, and perfect, which hath a beginning, a midst, and an end. So the place of any building may be whole and entire for that work, though too little for a palace. As to a tragedy or a comedy, the action may be convenient and perfect that would not fit an epic poem in magnitude. So a lion is a perfect creature in himself, though it be less than that of a buffalo or a rhinoceros. They differ but in specie: either in the kind is absolute; both have their parts, and either the whole. Therefore, as in every body so in every action, which is the subject of a just work, there is required a certain proportionable greatness, neither too vast nor too minute. For that which happens to the eyes when we behold a body, the same happens to the memory when we contemplate an action. I look upon a monstrous giant, as Tityus,[1] whose body covered nine acres of land, and mine eye sticks upon every part; the whole that consists of those parts will never be taken in at one entire view. So in a fable, if the action be too great, we can never comprehend the whole together in our imagination. Again, if it be too little, there ariseth no pleasure out of the object; it affords the view no stay; it is beheld, and vanisheth at once. As if we should look upon an ant or pismire,[2] the parts fly the sight, and the whole considered is almost nothing. The same happens in action, which is the object of memory, as the body is of sight. Too vast oppresseth the eyes, and exceeds the memory; too little scarce admits either.

Language most shows a man: Speak, that I may see thee. It springs out of the most retired and inmost parts of us, and is the image of the parent of it, the mind. No glass[3] renders a man's form or likeness so true as his speech. Nay, it is likened to a man; and as we consider feature and composition in a man, so words in language; in the greatness, aptness, sound structure, and harmony of it.

---

1   *Tityus*   Giant in Greek mythology.
2   *pismire*   Ant.
3   *glass*   Mirror.

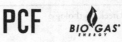